WORKING
THE
PLATE

ALSO BY MARTY APPEL

Baseball's Best: The Hall of Fame Gallery
(with Burt Goldblatt)

Thurman Munson: An Autobiography
(with Thurman Munson)

Batting Secrets of the Major Leaguers

Tom Seaver's All-Time Baseball Greats
(with Tom Seaver)

Hardball: The Education of a Baseball Commissioner
(as editorial assistant to Bowie Kuhn)

The First Book of Baseball

Yesterday's Heroes

Joe DiMaggio

WORKING
THE
PLATE
THE ERIC GREGG STORY

Eric Gregg and Marty Appel

William Morrow and Company, Inc.
New York

Recognizing the importance of preserving what has been written, it is the policy of William Morrow and Company, Inc., and its imprints and affiliates to have the books it publishes printed on acid-free paper, and we exert our best efforts to that end.

Library of Congress Cataloging-in-Publication Data

Gregg, Eric, 1951–
    Working the plate : the Eric Gregg story / Eric Gregg and Marty
Appel.
        p.   cm.
    ISBN 0-688-09089-3
    1. Gregg, Eric, 1951–   . 2. Baseball—United States—Umpires—
Biography. I. Appel, Martin. II. Title.
GV865.G685A3   1990
796.357′092—dc20   89-77642
[B]   CIP

Printed in the United States of America

First Edition

1 2 3 4 5 6 7 8 9 10

BOOK DESIGN BY J. PONSIGLIONE

To the late Barney Deary, who took me out of the ghetto, and to Conchita Gregg, who set me on the right path
—E.G.

To the memory of Robert O. Fishel
—M.A.

Contents

WORKING
THE
PLATE

CHAPTER ONE

Mary Sue

MARY SUE STYLES.

A great name, isn't it? A perfect name for, well, a ballgirl in Veterans Stadium, Philadelphia, my hometown. She was just the right mixture. Blond, skimpy little outfit, "All-American" wholesome good looks, just the proper level of rooting interest in the Phillies. Perfect.

I didn't know her last name at the time, but she was already a little famous in Philly as just "Mary Sue," the beautiful teenage ballgirl down the left field line. An equally attractive, but brunette counterpart handled right field.

I always loved working in my hometown, and although I certainly had no rooting interest, I was already getting a little bit of fame myself. The fans at the Vet recognized me and got on me from time to time. I enjoyed it. This was the city where I fell in love with baseball. To be standing there, on the major league diamond in front of my hometown neighbors . . . hey, it was heaven.

On September 29, 1979, we had the archrivals of Pennsylvania, the Pittsburgh Pirates, battling the Phils for an Eastern Division championship, and how nice it was to have this state go one-on-one with two great teams. I was out there working third base, pretty new to the league myself, just sort of marveling over how terrific things were going, when Keith Moreland, a rookie catcher with the Phils, comes up with the score tied 1–1.

Well, as bad luck would have it, Moreland lifts one deep down the line in left field. I know it's got the distance but does it have the foul line covered? It's going to be my call.

Now one of the little things that they teach you in umpire school has to do with night baseball and stadium lights. This is not something an average fan ever thinks about, but that's what umpire school is all about. You learn hundreds of situations that come up, things that nobody ever pays much attention to at all. And this particular lesson, which I chose to forget at that very moment, was that an umpire must never, ever, look up into the lights. Do it, and you're blind. It may only be for a second, but that precious second can cost you a call, and that call can cost a team a game. You just plain keep your eyes out of the lights.

I was not quite a rookie that night, but I made a rookie mistake. I followed the flight of the ball and looked right into the lights.

What do you know, the theory works. I'm blinded. And sure enough, I never see the ball go into the seats at all. Still, it's my call. Fair or foul, fair or foul. There are fifty players, forty thousand fans, a TV audience of a few hundred thousand, and three other umpires all looking at Eric Gregg.

This was no time to panic. And no time to look indecisive. I didn't see the ball, but I saw the next best thing. I saw Mary Sue jumping up and down with more enthusiasm than I'd seen in a long time. I was checking out sweet Mary Sue, thigh high, and I said to myself, "Eric, if it's good enough for Mary Sue, it's good enough for you."

"Home run," I yelled, twirling my finger in the air in a signal that meant, "touch 'em all." The tie was broken, the Phillies went out in front, and Moreland had his first major league home run.

Instantly, the Pirates charged me from all corners of the field. I don't think Moreland was even at second base yet. Here came their two tanks, Dave Parker from right and Willie Stargell from first, 450 pounds on the run. Talk about the Indians surrounding the wagon train . . . I was the lead wagon.

It did occur to me at this point that I might have blown it, but I was still prepared to think it was real close and this was a normal Pirate reaction. After all, would Mary Sue have gotten so excited if it was foul?

I held my ground, but then that crazy shortstop, Tim Foli, who was never any good to umpires, came screaming at me like a rooster yelling, "Did you see it? Did you see it?" I chose not to answer, probably another mistake, because he immediately interpreted that as a "no," and went running to all his teammates yelling, "He didn't see it, he didn't see it!"

Things were starting to get a little tense. Fortunately, at this point at least, this was all good news to the fans, so they were cheering away up in the stands, and not causing any other problems.

It was obvious that I needed a little conference with my fellow umpires, most of all with our crew chief, Doug Harvey.

Doug was about fifty then, but his white hair made him seem older, and he had this very proper, distinguished manner on the field that made him very much a father figure to young umpires like myself. He had been in the National League since 1962, and had won arguments with no less than Casey Stengel, Leo Durocher, and Walter Alston over the years. Doug could handle it.

"What's up, kid?" he asked, as the four of us converged.

I went straight to the heart of the matter.

"Chief," I said, "I didn't see it."

"No shit," he answered.

I had a feeling now that maybe it wasn't close.

"What are you going to do?" Harvey wanted to know. Under the circumstances, I thought he was remarkably calm. The Pirates were clustered just a few feet away, and changing the call would get a lot of people on the other side furious. But he had asked me the right question. It was Eric Gregg's call. There was no way Doug would overrule me. But he had given me the opportunity to think it through with my partners, and had given me an opening to get his counsel.

"Chief," I answered, "if I saw the play, I'd stick by my call. Right or wrong, I've got to trust my judgment. But I didn't see it. All I saw was Mary Sue jumping up and down, and she convinced me it was fair."

"Well, kid," said Harvey, "if the ball's fair, it's got to hit the screen and kick back. I didn't see it hit the screen, and we know it didn't bounce back."

He looked patiently at my other two partners.

"Did either of you guys see it hit the screen?"

Both said no. They knew that shaking their heads would be a bad sign to the players and fans, so they spoke.

So I said, "Then let's get it right then. Let's change it."

Harvey said, "Do you want to make the change, kid?"

I sized up the situation, looked at the forty thousand celebrating Phillies fans, and decided to say, "Doug, you change it."

He did. He signaled "foul ball," we took three runs off the board for Philadelphia, and you never saw anything like it. Dallas Green, the Phillies manager, led the charge from the dugout, with Larry Bowa, the Phils' answer to Foli, right behind him. Poor Moreland, his first major league homer gone, and the sounds of forty thousand pretty aggravated customers are ringing those big liberty bells in deep center. It was awful, but I heard them out, threw Green and Bowa out for going too far with their arguments, and waited out the furor. At last, peace was restored.

Luck was with me, as it happened. The Phillies rallied to win after all, and the next day, in the newspapers, Stargell said, "I tip my cap to Eric Gregg. He obviously didn't see that ball, but he made sure that in the end he got it right."

By the next day, Mary Sue Styles and I were celebrities. I learned her last name during the postgame press interviews I had to give, and I think we were forever joined in Phillies history.

Up until that point, only a few people knew that this umpire, the only black umpire in the league, was from Philly. Now, the whole city met me. Since then, I've never made an appearance in that city without someone saying "Hey, Eric, how about that Keith Moreland home run and Mary Sue Styles?"

The newfound celebrity led to my getting my own spot on local television, my own TV commercials, and lots of speaking engagements.

It wasn't long before I was dancing with the Phillies Phanatic mascot to pass the time between innings, having a laugh or two, and entertaining the fans.

People would say to me, "Eric, how come you're the only umpire who dances with the Phillies Phanatic?"

"That's easy," I say. "I'm the only umpire who can dance!"

CHAPTER TWO

The Bottom

WHAT CAN YOU say about a life that starts out at the Bottom?

Nowhere to go but up would be the obvious answer, but most don't make it out. That cliché really doesn't work.

The Bottom is a neighborhood in West Philadelphia, a nickname for a bunch of crossing streets that only those who live there generally use. Most Philadelphia natives don't even know about the nickname. It's all just "West Philly" to them.

Number 616 North Pallas Street was on the fringes of The Bottom, between Haverford Avenue and Wallace Street. I was born there. Route 76 and the Schuylkill River cut us off from downtown Philly, but you could take the 33 bus to Spring Garden and the 30 to Dobbins High, a block from the old Connie Mack Stadium.

We call it The Bottom because there was not much room for optimism. Most of the adults we came into contact with had long ago given up high hopes or aspirations. The ghetto attitude had beaten them down. There was little talk about "study hard and go far," or "you can be anything you want to be." There was no "American dream" at The Bottom. There was just the daily routine of seeing things through, making ends meet, and getting from one day to the next. If truancy was the way of life for school kids, adults didn't have a very convincing way of disciplining it out of their system. The available jobs were low-end and not much better than welfare. Role models just weren't there, unless your young impressionable head would be turned by the pimps or drug pushers in their stylish clothing and expensive cars. The system in general had you marked for failure from the start.

At least I knew my heritage. My father was Ernest E. Gregg, born on June 23, 1925, in Philadelphia. His father, also named Ernest, was from Richmond, Virginia, and was born in 1907. He married a Philadelphia girl named Violet, and drove a sanitation truck for the City of Philadelphia for forty years. He had a lot of watches as I recall—some he had fished out of the garbage, and two that had been given to him for long service to the city.

My mother, Dorothy Mae Ginyard, was also born in Philadelphia—March 19, 1929. Her parents came from North Carolina. Her mother's name was Ollie.

That my father was able to maintain a steady job for thirty-five years was kind of amazing, because he was not what you'd call a steady, reliable person. But for thirty-five years he worked as a shipper for the Garrett Buchanan Paper Company, and although he had only a small income, it was one constant in our lives.

My mother supplemented that by working as a beautician out of our kitchen. Black women would come right to the house to get their hair fried and straightened. There was always a little black-and-white television set going while she went about her business, and it was always tuned to the soap operas. As a result, since I was thirteen years old, I've been addicted to the soaps, and still follow them faithfully every day. If I could trade in my baseball career for something else, it would only be as an actor in a soap.

The soaps were a great escape. Right there, right on the little black-and-white set in our own kitchen, people were playing out scenes from white America that seemed so far removed from our lives. The characters were middle class, upper middle, or upper, but all of the little touches—the clothing, the appliances, the references to travel and jobs, were all right there in front of us, telling us what they had that we didn't.

Still, I really had no complaints. I would have liked to have lived in a nicer neighborhood, had a nicer house, aspired to a college education, and to live out those soap opera luxuries. But I actually think back now and see I had a happy childhood. I don't remember lacking clothes, or sneakers, or any special toys. I had friends, I liked to have fun, play ball, hang out, and I even liked school. I wasn't the world's greatest student, but I liked certain teachers, certain classes, and the social life that school gave us. I made the most of it.

I liked my little neighborhood. Lancaster Avenue was *The* Avenue, to the people of The Bottom. Fifty-second Street is The Strip. The Bottom ran from around Thirty-third Street to Forty-fourth. But all the little side streets had special memories. Our food market, our Laundromat, my old bicycle shop, the five-and-ten, my aunt's house, my uncle, who was the first one to get a new RCA color television set around 1965, the post office, even Pat's Hoagies. Pat's been there for forty years. I went there as a kid, and I still stop by now, except now he's got my photo on the wall. And now, he's got a grating between the counter and the customers after too many close calls, and some not so close. Pat's white, and it hasn't been easy for him at times in an all-black neighborhood. But he makes a great hoagie.

On Pallas Street we had a guy with one arm who was always chasing us for stealing grapes off his vine. And we had an old Indian woman who ran after us with an axe. And there was Mrs. Brown, who had a dog that looked just like Lassie.

Michael Jones was one of my early friends, and probably my first hero. A great basketball player from the neighborhood, he even went to college and played basketball, graduated in four years, and went on to play pro basketball in Italy. When he finally returned home, he realized that he had a degree, but he didn't have an education to go with it. His experience was exactly what is suddenly being discovered at colleges throughout the country. All Michael Jones was at college for was bas-ketball. They didn't give him an education; they just passed him through his classes so he'd remain eligible for the team. He could have learned a trade in those four years; could have prepared himself for the likeli-hood that he wouldn't be a star in the NBA. But the school looked the other way. They wanted those re-bounds and didn't care about Michael Jones five years later. Today, he's got a hot dog stand on the corner in The Bottom. I see him whenever I'm home. He shouldn't be doing that now, but that's what the educational sys-tem had in mind for Michael in the seventies whether they knew it or not.

My grandmother lived at Forty-fourth and Fair-mont, until one day, her little house just collapsed. Just like that, thud, down it came. Luckily, no one was there at the time. And now it's just a vacant space between two other row houses, as though no one ever lived there.

Just around from that house, and diagonally across

the street from mine, was a lot next to the church that served as a baseball field for us. Actually, two fields. It was L-shaped, and you could only imagine diamonds in your mind. It was a combination of rock and dirt, concrete and blacktop, weeds and trees. Somehow, we figured out the configuration for baseball fields.

First base was the pole. Second base was the tree. Third was another pole. A rock was home plate. We'd use a rubber ball or a wiffle ball, and the smaller kids would play closest to Pallas Street, the older kids backed up near where my grandmother lived.

I hit sixty home runs on the big lot to set a record. There was this clapboard hut in the corner of the lot, next to the church, and if you hit it onto the roof it was a double, and over the roof, a home run. The problem was, the nuns would always be chasing us out because the home runs were always winding up in the churchyard. And many is the time I'd just wander to this little lot, sit on a tree stump, and dream of playing big league baseball.

I remember the Phillies of the late fifties and early sixties. Now those were terrible teams. Last place almost every year, and still trying to remind you about the wonderful Whiz Kids of 1950, like it was going to happen again any day now. You had to be a strong fan to root for those dreadful Phillie teams then, but I was. In fact, I loved them. When I was ten years old, maybe the greatest age of all to be a baseball fan, my Phillies lost twenty-three games in a row. They finished forty-six games out of first, and seventeen games out of ninth. Most of the country was watching Mickey Mantle and Roger Maris belt all of those home runs in 1961, but for those of us in Philly, it was the summer of that great losing streak, the summer of Gene Mauch, and Art Mahaffey, Ruben Amaro and Tony Taylor, Tony Gonzalez

and Pancho Herrera, Frank Sullivan and John Buz-
hardt, Johnny Callison and Clay Dalrymple, Jack Bald-
schun and Dallas Green. It was a summer in which we
hung on every game, waiting to see if the Phils would
ever win again.

Actually, from that awful team came a lot of players
who just three years later almost won the National
League pennant. But if you were a Phillies fan, you knew
about heartache. And in 1964 came the collapse to end
all collapses. They had a lock on the pennant, so it
seemed, and then suddenly, just as we were preparing
for a World Series, and just as I was trying my best to
figure out how I'd get enough money to buy a World
Series ticket, the Phils lost ten games in a row and blew
the whole thing. St. Louis won the pennant, and I sat
there in the kitchen, watching the Cardinals play the
Yankees in the World Series and trying to come to terms
with what had gone wrong. For those of us who lived
through it, we're still looking for the answers. But that
was what it meant to be a Phillies fan. That was my
heritage in baseball. I came from The Bottom and I
rooted for the Phillies and I lived through the 1964
screwup. Was this any way to go out into the world?

I was a bigger fan than most of my friends. In fact,
many was the time I couldn't get anyone to go to the
games with me, so I went alone. Not too many black
people went to games, not then, and still not today. I'd
get a dollar and a half from my mother and a buck from
my dad to go to the game. I'd go maybe forty times a
year. I had my system down. The busfare was thirty
cents, but if I dropped in fifteen pennies, the driver
would never count them, and I'd be fifteen cents to the
good. If you got there late enough, the ticket takers would
let you in for free after the game was well under way.
I'd have enough money left for an extra hot dog. And
I'd sit there in a vacant seat, rooting for the Phillies to

pull one out, and dreaming of being a major leaguer myself one day, maybe even wearing those handsome red pinstripes with the huge numbers on the backs.

I met my first real major league umpire on one of those summer afternoons at Connie Mack Stadium. Ed Sudol came over to me outside the park after a game and asked if I was the kid who'd been stealing the wheels off his car.

Karen was my oldest sister, born in 1948. Cheryl was born thirteen months later. I was born on May 18, 1951, and my brother Ernest was born February 28, 1953. The two girls made it through the eleventh grade before they quit school. Neither one got married. Ernie was a real hustle guy and never went to school very much. He was a street gang guy, always getting into fights. He somehow got as far as ninth grade. I wish I had his height. He grew to be six-seven, and if I put my weight on that frame, I'd be doing fine. Ernie, Cheryl, and Karen were not untypical of kids raised around The Bottom. They were subjected to a lot of things and victimized by a lot of what they saw. I wish I still had the three of them at my side today to share in my success. But it hasn't turned out that way at all. Ernie's doing time, Karen's just getting by, and Cheryl . . . well, we lost Cheryl to drugs a couple of years ago. More on all of that later.

Dad had his problems too. He drank too much, and he was a violent man. All too often he would leave a chunk of his paycheck in the neighborhood saloons. He would come home on those occasions looking for trouble. You knew it as soon as he walked into the house. The slightest thing could set him off.

Was dinner late? Was it not cooked just right? Oh my, how he'd get into a rage.

And he'd hit my mother. Those are the worst childhood memories for me. I'd be in bed, but the door would be open enough for me to see out. And wham!, he'd belt her with an open hand. Wham! They were slaps, not punches, and I suppose something in his mind made him keep his fist from forming, but he didn't hold back on the slaps. And my mother would yell at him to stop, yell out that he shouldn't do this in front of the children, and she'd cry, and he'd go out. They were awful moments for a little boy.

Now in many black families, the father splits. Sooner or later, defeated in his quest to provide for his family, humiliated by his status in life, he takes off. That didn't happen in my house. At my house, my mother finally worked up the courage to make the move. This was very unusual. In the first place, it was her house. It had been her parents', and they gave it to my folks when they got married.

Number 616 North Pallas was a row house, attached to a block of about twenty similar houses, all different colors. My dad still lives there today, and the rusty screen door with the G in the center can still swing in the breeze. There's a comfortable front porch there with a couple of metal chairs for passing the time.

When Mom took us away from that little row house, we split up for a time. My two sisters moved into the projects with Aunt Wil, and Ernie and I lived with Aunt Vivian on Redfield Street. This was until Mom found a place for us all at 1702 North Redfield Street. I was only fourteen. It was a tough time to have the family split up, but already, my sisters were pretty much coming and going as they chose to.

Although the family wasn't together anymore, I was still close to my grandparents, my father's parents. They were great to me, and I spent a lot of time at their place. Sundays were especially fine times there, with these great breakfast feasts. My grandmother always managed to scrape together five dollars for a birthday present for me, and you know, even when I was in the major leagues, a married man, she would still send me five dollars for my birthday.

I was known as "Hub" ever since I was just eight or nine years old. I can tell when someone from the neighborhood calls to me at a ball game, because they still call me Hub. A guy named Willis gave me the nickname. He got this idea somehow that I was trying to steal hubcaps off his father's car. I said to him, "I don't even have a car, Willis. What am I gonna do with hubcaps?"

Of course, the fact that he caught me in the act of actually prying them off was hardly a reason to confess.

"Well from now on," he said, "I'm just gonna call you Hub." And he did, and soon, so did everyone. Even at my high school reunion in 1988, I was introduced as "Hub."

I went to the Martha Washington School in the early grades, a traditional-looking inner-city school, built in 1929, across the street from where the projects are today.

When it came time for junior high, I was smart enough to know that the neighborhood school was nothing but a dead end. I mean, it was trouble. I saw nothing good there, only kids in trouble, kids thinking about trouble, and trouble sitting there all by itself waiting for kids to walk over. And somehow, even at that early age, I knew that I had to get away from this particular school.

So all by myself, I faked my home address, and enrolled across town at Anna Howard Shaw Junior High. Shaw was half black, half white, and much better any way you cut it. Everyone knew it, but not everyone at my age would have the guts to take city buses across town every day and fake an address like I did. I think back now and smile and tell myself, "That was a gutsy little move for a thirteen-year-old kid."

I started taking odd jobs when I was in junior high. For years I delivered *The Philadelphia Inquirer*. I also shined shoes outside a famous beer garden a few blocks from my house. It was called Raleigh's, and I remember making ten dollars on my biggest day. I used to see my dad there a lot too. It was a classy-looking old saloon with that thick translucent glass forming part of the outer wall. I never did go inside in all the time I camped out there, giving those fifteen-cent shines. Ten dollars meant I did more than sixty shines in one day, and usually I was only there for a couple of hours on days when there was no school.

I also earned some money busing tables. It was at a diner called "5218," which was, of course, its street address. It's a park today. My sister Cheryl waitressed there from time to time.

In ninth grade I started dating a pretty girl named Marcelle Ancrum. She was a little older than I was. I had skipped a grade in elementary school, and was one of the youngest kids in my class. They had a 4A and a 4B class, and I was skipped over 4B and moved into fifth grade. What that did was make me kind of shy and insecure, because in those early grades, even a few months' difference can mean a lot. And Marcelle, being several months older than I was, frightened me just a little. We dated off and on for two years, and she was as close to having a real girlfriend as I got. I took her to my junior prom, but a year later, I was into one of those shy periods with her, and I was nervous about asking her to the senior prom. By the time I got up my nerve, she had already accepted another date.

My two best male friends were Carl Cooper and

Earl Timbers. I think Earl became an inhalation thera-
pist at a local hospital. Carl was maybe more typical of
the neighborhood. I visited him last year at Holmsberg
Prison. He was in on some drug and burglary charges,
which he said he had nothing to do with.

My mom tried her best to get us all to apply ourselves in school, but she had her own problems making
ends meet, she had that awful relationship with my father, and well, there was only so much you could do.
She never really paid much attention to whether we were
getting home on time and things like that. I wish I could
look back and recall a lot of closeness, a lot of affection
in my home. It just wasn't my parents' nature. I know
they loved us, but they just weren't all that good at
showing it. I guess the daily struggles took a little of
that tenderness out of people. I have no recollection at
all of sitting on my folks' laps, having them tell me a
story, or just hugging and snuggling. It's something I
make sure we have in my home today.

I was five-seven and 165 pounds when I entered
tenth grade at West Philadelphia High. I had started
out at Overbrook High, lying about my address again to
go to what I thought was a better school. But I missed
Marcelle and other friends who went to West Philly, so
I transferred myself back to where I belonged. Baseball
still meant more to me than anything. Playing it and
watching it. I still loved the Phillies, and by now, Richie Allen had joined the team and was their biggest
star. I loved Richie. He could mash the baseball, and
he had some style too. The press was always on him,
and the fans booed him a lot, but in Philadelphia, as
they say, the fans would boo a funeral. And Richie could
give it back. I was sitting there on days that he'd scratch
a big BOO into the dirt at first base in answer to the
fans. One day he scratched MVP, casting his vote early

and doing a little campaigning. He didn't win. You had to understand Richie Allen. He was kind of a brash black star, at a time when people were still not sure what to do about a guy like that. Some of his teammates were still raised in times where black people "knew their place." Richie knew his all right, but it wasn't what white folks had in mind for him. So he offended a lot of people by being a free thinker. Eventually, he became the highest-paid player in the game, and you'd have to say he did it his way.

I'm not sure if I admired him as much for his boldness as for his fantastic ability. He swung the heaviest bat in the majors and could really apply power to that little baseball. Since I was neither a militant nor an activist, I suspect my admiration was for his playing ability, with a little youthful rebellion set aside to admire a guy who traveled his own roads.

Tom Jacoby was Eric's junior varsity baseball coach at West Philadelphia High School.

"In the late 1960s, Philadelphia was a lot like other big cities. There was a lot of black awareness developing, with many students leaning towards militancy, and many taking a more wait-and-see approach. We had bad riots on Columbia Avenue in the northern part of the city when much of the rest of the nation went through those times too.

"Drugs weren't really a problem yet. I'd say the big thing was the street gangs. There were a lot of gang problems at the school, and even walking there in the mornings could be a challenge. You had to be careful of who you made eye contact with, whether you smiled when you weren't supposed to, whether you looked at someone else's girlfriend the wrong way. They were tense times. I think in many ways the coming of the drug period ended the era of the fighting street gangs, only because the drugs would put them in a stupor and take the fight out of them. Not that that's gaining anything, I suppose.

"West Philly High was pretty much a mixed bag when Hub went to school here. It was all black, but mixed in terms of class. You had some middle class blacks, and some just down and out. We had a pretty high dropout rate. I never knew Hub's brother or sisters because they were early dropouts.

"The down and outs were the tough ones. The middle class, which included Hub, had to learn to be diplomats, how to hold their own, when to smile, when to be aggressive. A lot of this prepared him for umpiring I'm sure.

"I loved having Hub come out for baseball. He was so coachable that he was a delight. And he was so likable that you'd almost want to take him home and adopt him. He really learned the mechanics of the game so well. You'd show him how to position his feet when he batted, and he'd pick it up in a second. He learned so quickly and never forgot.

"Unfortunately, his weight was already a problem. He must have been like five-one and 210 pounds.

"He was the kind of kid who'd do everything right at the plate and line a clean base hit to right field. But he'd be so slow, they'd throw him out at first just the same. And when that happened, he'd actually start to cry. Real tears. He loved the game so much, but it was so frustrating for him to get it right and then still not have it come out the way it should have. But he was a coach's dream. And he wanted to get out of the ghetto so badly."

My varsity coach at West Philadelphia High, Joe Goldenberg, looked at me one day and said, "Eric, I've got to be honest with you. If you can't play ball for the

West Philly Speed Boys, there's no way you're gonna play for the Phillies."

Up to that point, I kind of always thought that I might actually be a big league player. After all, I had those sixty home runs on the lot off Pallas Street, and I seemed much more into the game than my friends were. I sort of reasoned that that was all it took. The coach's words shook me up. But when you think about it, I was barely the third-string catcher on the team, and I suppose most major leaguers have a more distinguished high school record.

Just around that time, what you'd call the biggest moment in my life took place. If I had become a priest, I would say it was the moment when I got "the calling." If I had become a doctor, I would say it was the first time I ever visited a doctor's office and felt that I too could save a life someday.

I was sitting home on this particular Saturday afternoon, watching *The Game of the Week* on NBC. The Phillies were playing, and it wasn't often they were on *The Game of the Week*, so it had my attention. Curt Gowdy was broadcasting, and at a break in the action, he read a promotional announcement prepared by Major League Baseball for a quick drop-in during the game.

"Become a major league umpire," he said. "Make thirty thousand dollars a year. For information, write to Umpire Development School, St. Petersburg, Florida."

I sat up straight in my chair. Thirty thousand dollars sounded like a fortune. More than my father ever made, I was sure. And, he said "major leagues." Could this be for me?

I'm sure that each week, somebody in the baseball commissioner's office types out these "promos" to be read on *The Game of the Week*. I guess that a small percentage of people actually listen when the announcer

reads them. Whoever it was who typed out the umpire
school promotional announcement should know that today, they're responsible for one major league umpire.

The fact that I was only seventeen didn't even occur to me. In my neighborhood, you grew up fast. If I
could take buses across town to junior high, I could find
my way to Florida.

I wrote down the address and got off a letter to the
school, asking for more information. I had to see if it
cost anything, and how soon I had to apply.

Even before I got a response, I knew I had to speak
to them. I couldn't wait for a form letter in the mail.

By this time I had another part-time job, working at
Phototype Engraving Company. They had a phone you
could dial long distance on, and I tracked down the
number for Umpire Development School and called.

I reached a man named Barney Deary. I asked to
speak to the person in charge, and he told me that I was
speaking to him. I guess it was a fairly small operation.
His wife was the secretary.

I told him about hearing Curt Gowdy, and that I
wanted to be an umpire.

Mr. Deary gave me some of the particulars, including that I had to be twenty-one years old. I was a little
shy of this, about four years.

"Well son," he said, "there's no way we can take a
seventeen-year-old boy down here. But I've got a lot of
friends in the Philadelphia area. How about if I get you
involved in Little League umpiring, just to get you going.
And maybe if you find you enjoy it, we can talk again
when you're twenty-one."

And true to his word, he made some calls, and arranged for me to umpire in Little League games. And
that was my start in umpiring, and my start of a relationship with a great man named Barney Deary.

Before you knew it, I was umping Little League baseball for six- and seven-year-old kids. I got about eight dollars a game, which was not bad money in 1967.

I always got along well with little children, and even today, when they come to the park and see me dancing with the mascots, they take to me. I love watching kids have a great time at a ballpark.

I really enjoyed the Little League experience and the feelings that were coming over me on the field. Part of it, I'm sure, was the importance of umpiring. Whereas I might have taken some of it for granted before, now I was keenly aware of the power of the umpire. Even if you performed in a quiet, nonflamboyant way, you were conducting the flow of the game. You were the authority on rules and interpretations of rules, and believe me, in Little League, you saw everything. It was a solid beginning.

Oh, you had your share of "Little League Parents," those wonderful folks who come to see their kids in action and start getting on the umpires. Imagine that! Imagine what a terrible example that was setting for those kids in how to deal with an authority figure. Some of those parents would embarrass themselves so badly, their kids would walk over to me and apologize for them.

It was an all-white neighborhood I worked in, but I never had any problem with the kids. I always had their respect and never heard a single racial remark from them. I was the only black person in the program; all the other umpires were white.

The fields were nicely kept, had outfield fences, and I wore a real umpire's uniform, complete with blue pants, a blue shirt, a cap and a tie. I didn't like the ties very much, and I'm delighted that they aren't a part of an umpire's uniform today. But the look then made me feel like an authority figure and I think it made me bear down more and become very good at umpiring.

It was a treat to see the kids developing their skills, learning the rules, having a good, wholesome time. Sometimes they'd be so into the game, they'd do the most absent-minded things. On more than one occasion, the pitcher would deliver the baseball while the catcher was out of the box, and plunk me with the ball when I wasn't expecting it. I'd warn them not to do it again, but it was just absentmindedness, and it was hard to get mad, even after a hardball in the thigh.

One day we had this little kid named Billy, and his team was losing by something like 21–1, one of those typical Little League scores. It was just awful.

As Billy came to bat in the last inning, tears were running down his cheeks. The count went to three-and-two, when he turned to me and asked for time. Seven years old, mind you.

He looked up at me and said, "Mister, you see that guy coaching third base? That's my dad. I've struck out three times today, and if I strike out again, he's really gonna let me have it."

What could you do?

So the next pitch comes in near the corner, close enough, probably a strike, but I call it ball four. He walks, a run scores, and his team loses 21–2. What the hell.

A week later, I'm waiting for another game to start. I'm talking to the umpires from the other fields, and I tell them the story about Billy.

Together, they all say, "Billy! That kid get you too? He pulls that shit every week! You didn't get him a free walk, did you?"

It was my first lesson in umpiring. From a seven-year-old.

My class at West Philly High had about 800 students in it, almost all black, and I think I finished 799th. My favorite teachers were Mrs. Gee, who taught math, and Mr. Goldenberg, our baseball coach and gym teacher, who was pretty much a legend in Philly. He's the basketball coach now, and he's won, I believe, five championships for the school in basketball. I played baseball for him, sort of. I had two at bats in four seasons.

These were tense times in a ghetto community. In 1968, Dr. Martin Luther King, Jr., was assassinated. This came at a time when I believed things were going to get better. It may have been naïve on my part; I was still just a kid, but there was an optimism in the air, a feeling that things were going to be better for my generation than it had been for my parents and my grandparents.

A lot of my friends wanted to take to the streets and riot when Dr. King was killed. We were at a school dance when the news came. My friends wanted to break some windows and tear open the school. I thought that was bull. It was certainly not the way Dr. King would have wanted it. This wasn't white America going to war with black America. This was one cracker redneck perpetrating an ignorant crime. There was no way I thought that required burning down the little that we had in West Philadelphia. This was our school. What would we gain by destroying it? A lot of my friends went the black power way after the events of 1968, but I never did. We argued over it. Maybe seeing my parents fight all the time made me more of a peace-loving person. But I've never changed in all of these years, never had a desire to see violence. Even when I was young and could be swayed by my friends, I held firm to Dr. King's values. I still do.

My best subjects in school were art and wood shop, and I was in the dance club. I even got my friends Fred Stokes and Bill Jones to join up. They were real macho types, but I talked them into joining, and soon some others did too, and we had a great time and a great group. We performed *Bye Bye Birdie* and I was in the chorus as a dancer. We not only performed in our school, but toured the city and performed it at other schools too. By now I was five-nine and about 180, growing every day, and I know the highlight of *Bye Bye Birdie* was when we performed it at an elementary school and I was in a squat position and I couldn't get up. The other dancers had to kind of hoist me back into line, and that got a terrific reaction from those little kids.

Of course, high school was not without its moments of trouble. I suppose the worst of all came from drinking Boone's Farm and Thunderbird wine. Carl Cooper and I and some of the other guys would get our twenty-five or thirty cents together and hang out and drink this stuff. We were good drunks, mind you, not problem drunks, but still, we were underage. We'd tank up and start harmonizing some of those great sixties tunes out of Motown, songs by Marvin Gaye, Otis Redding, and the Temptations.

One day, we drank too much and sang too loud, and the cops found us in the gym at the Y. It was about eleven P.M. and they crashed into the room and scared the hell out of us. It was hands up against the wall and everything, just like on TV. And they hauled us into a paddy wagon for a trip to the police station.

Big hero that I was, I actually started to cry. Not so much because we were going to jail, but because I had a Popsicle in my pocket and it was starting to melt, and in all the confusion, I didn't know what to do with it. But one of the guys said, "Hey, don't cry, I'll eat your Popsicle," and he did, cool as can be, right in the back of the paddy wagon like nothing was wrong.

When we got to the station house, it was pretty scary. There were some real criminals hanging around waiting to be booked, and one cop muttered to us that "you might get five years for this." I believed him. These were the days when Frank Rizzo ran the Philadelphia police department, and he had a very tough reputation in black communities. It helped him to get elected mayor of Philadelphia not long afterward. I even figured out how old I would be when I got out, and wondered if they'd still take me in umpire school at that age, and with this criminal record.

Well, we're wasting away in the detention cell for what seemed like weeks, but about three in the morning, after three hours in the slammer, my mother and Coop's mother arrived. It was definitely the longest night of my life, and I swore up and down that I'd never drink again.

Of course, what I really meant was that I'd never get caught again. It wasn't long before we had our courage back and would go off guzzling again once in a while.

One night, we were hiding out in the girls' gym, guzzling some cheap wine as usual, when we heard someone coming. During our escape, Earl Timbers cut himself on a window, and the blood left a trail, and one girl identified us by Earl's cut. That led to a week's suspension from school.

There was one other police incident. It involved shooting off firecrackers in the neighborhood. We heard the police coming and I ran up and hid under my bed. The police came to the door, my mother answered, and shouted up to my room, "Hub, are you up there?" I still remember that, because she didn't know I was. So I was hiding out from the police and lying to my mom, but I got away with it. When my mom reads this book, it will be the first time she'll ever discover the truth about that day.

All in all, not a very bad record for someone from The Bottom. I survived it.

When I was eighteen, I entered a contest sponsored by Gillette in which I had to say why I liked using their razor blades.

Of course, I didn't even shave then, but that didn't stop me from entering. First prize was a trip to the Super Bowl in Miami.

As I said, I wasn't the greatest student in West Philadelphia High School, but as they say, when the going gets tough the tough get going. I wrote the essay of my life, fifty words or less. I talked about the fact that my father used some other blade and was always getting nicked, but that since I switched to Gillette, I never got cut, and they lasted for weeks.

As luck would have it, not only did I win the trip, but so did the New York Jets, my favorite football team at the time. Joe Namath was my favorite player. We were both going to the Super Bowl!

Namath had been my favorite even when he was in college. In fact, besides dreaming that I could play major league baseball, my other goal was to be a quarterback for the University of Alabama. I'm not sure if Alabama was ready for a black quarterback, but Bear Bryant could have had one eager one on his squad if he'd only discovered me.

Although the winner got two tickets, I couldn't find anybody to go with. I didn't have a girlfriend at the time, and even if I did, we were a little young to go away together. Ernie was more into trouble than football, and none of my friends thought it was such a big deal. Also, even though it was a free trip, you had to have some pocket money with you, and my friends were just too poor to think about such a big event. I had a trip for two, and had to go by myself.

No problem. When you're from The Bottom, you handle things. It was a tough neighborhood.

At the engraving company, I couldn't hold back my excitement. I told everyone the Jets would win, even though the NFL had clobbered the AFL in the first two Super Bowls. People thought I was crazy, but here I was, sixteen (I said I was eighteen to enter the contest), and off I went to Miami.

Everybody told me to sit in the back when they took me to the airport, but I couldn't help noticing the wide comfy seats near the front of the plane. I asked the stewardess what they were all about.

"Oh," she said, "that's first class."

"You mean first come, first serve?" I asked. She laughed and laughed as though I was so clever, and I laughed along with her, but it was a serious question, and she never did answer me. For a long time, I thought first class meant first come, first served.

In Miami I stayed at the Cadillac Hotel, and made friends with a little Puerto Rican kid and his dad. I loved the climate, enjoyed walking around and seeing the palm trees, and of course, I loved the game, which the Jets won 16–7 behind Namath, making me look like a genius when I got home.

CHAPTER THREE

Umpire School

I UMPIRED IN the Philadelphia Little League program for two years, and then I called Barney Deary again.

If he liked hearing from me or not, I couldn't tell, but he remembered me, and asked me all about my experiences in Little League.

Again I asked him about going to umpire school. I was eighteen now, getting ready to graduate high school, and I'd made up my mind that umpire school was my ambition. The age limit had been reduced from twenty-one to nineteen.

There must have been something in my plea that got to Barney.

"How old did you say you were now, Eric?"

"Eighteen," I answered. "Getting ready to graduate high school."

"Well, when are you gonna be nineteen?" he asked.

"May eighteenth," I told him.

"All right Eric, you'll turn nineteen once you're here, I guess we can make a little exception. Come on down."

I was in. I loaded up my '62 Chevy Impala (it had cost $250), and was ready to head south.

But before I could leave I still had to attend my

high school graduation. I would be the first one in my family to pull this day off, and I wasn't about to miss it.

I felt very proud that day. As I said, I wasn't exactly called upon to deliver the valedictory speech, but I got there, got my education, and stood there before my family and my "main squeeze," Marcelle, and felt really good about myself. Besides, I had a goal, a destiny, a plan. I was not going to fold back into The Bottom, taking some dull low-paying job in the white section, or hanging out in the neighborhood hoping something interesting would come along. I had my invitation from Barney Deary, a tank full of gas, and a mind full of dreams. I had a one-in-a-million shot, and it was my ticket out.

Not everyone shared my high expectations. "Wait 'til they find out you're black," said my friends at the engraving company. "You're dead."

It is true, the history of baseball was not overrun with black umpires. And it hadn't occurred to me that Barney Deary might care about that. Whether he even knew I was black was not something I gave any thought to, although being from Philadelphia, and sounding the way I did, he may have known. Still, it never came up.

Would he really have a surprised reaction upon meeting me? I wondered a little bit as I drove south down 95. There was even a moment at which I thought it might be wise to pull over and telephone him and say something like, "Did I mention that I was black?" But then I realized how stupid that sounded and I was glad I didn't do anything that dumb.

There had been only one black major league umpire in 103 seasons of pro baseball by 1971. His name was Emmett Ashford, and he was fifty-two years old when the American League brought him up in 1966. He had spent fifteen years in the minors after spending

fifteen years with the Postal Service, so to say he had
paid his dues would be putting it mildly. He spent
twelve seasons in the Pacific Coast League before he
got the call. Finally, he broke one of the last remaining
color barriers in baseball, but it was obvious to everyone that he was a token selection, well past his prime,
and only a few years away from retirement.

Still, Emmett had a great zest for life and a wonderful spirit, and anyone who watched him during his
four seasons in the American League remembers him
as always hustling, often smiling, and always popular
with the fans. He was a bit of a showman, obviously
very noticeable, and a likable fellow.

The National League, which was always considered more progressive in hiring blacks, beginning
with Jackie Robinson in 1947, did not have a black umpire until 1973, after I'd completed umpire school. His
name was Art Williams.

Art had been a minor league player in the Tiger
organization when he switched to umpiring. He spent
four years umpiring in the minors before pressure to
bring up a black ump mounted and the National League
turned to him. Although I wasn't on the scene, I think
it's possible to assume that Art was rushed up a little
too quickly because of the pressure, and may not have
been ready. After five seasons, he was fired. The league
office said it was for "incompetence after many warnings."

Fifteen white umpires signed a petition to retain
him, which they likely would not have done if he was
truly an incompetent umpire, but again, I wasn't there
and I don't know all of the circumstances. He went on
welfare, then became a bus driver, and died at the age
of forty-four on the operating table from a brain tumor.
It was a pretty sad story.

But that was what I was driving down to in 1969—

one black umpire, Emmett Ashford, was the entire history to that point of black umpires who made good.

As for me and the '62 Chevy Impala, only one of us
made it all the way to Florida. I had my Auto Club maps
and was doing just fine, until smoke started to come out
of the engine around Georgia. I was only eight hours
out of Philly and this was not good. My car was falling apart, and I'd just had a $29.95 Earl Scheib paint
job too.

The guy at the gas station told me it would take five
hundred dollars to fix it. So long Impala.

I called my mom and she sent me an airline ticket
from Atlanta to St. Petersburg. It couldn't have been an
easy expense for her, but she came through for me.

The day I arrived, I put on my best plaid suit and
matching plaid hat and headed for the school's headquarters on 58 Ave. South and Gulfport Road. I arrived
with another student, Dave Pallone, and we were met
by Nick Bremigan, a first-year instructor.

He took one look at me and said, "You're Gregg."

I was shocked, which I suppose was an over-
reaction.

"How'd you know I was Gregg?" I asked him.

"How many black umpires do you think we've got
here?" he asked. "Plus, you're wearing a funny suit, so
you must be from Philadelphia."

Nick was a good man. I never forgot how welcome
he made me feel with that funny greeting. I would have
liked to have worked with him over the years, but our
paths took us to different leagues. He made the American League in 1974 and was a damn fine umpire. He
was an instructor even though his pro experience to that
point had only been two years in the Florida State
League and Florida Instructional League. He also spoke
a new language to me, "Baseball Vernacular." I thought

I knew the game, but Nick knew all the expressions unique to the sport.

Nick died during spring training of 1989 at his home in Garland, Texas, during a vacation break. He had a heart attack and was only forty-three. The odd thing was, he was a real health freak, a guy who really took care of himself. He played racquetball, lifted weights, rode bicycles, and swam. He never even rode elevators in hotels—he always walked.

I went to his funeral a few days later, although most of those in attendance were his American League partners. But I wanted to be there to see him off. I never forgot how he made me feel so comfortable that very first day.

The Umpire Development School, or Program, was fairly new when I arrived. It was begun in 1969 when I first applied. The politics behind it all was that the major leagues had decided that funding their own development programs was the wise course of action for producing future umpires. The first umpire school was begun in 1935 by George Barr. There had been other, privately run umpire schools, mostly in Florida, which had supplied umpires to the pros. The best-known had been the Bill McGowan Umpire School in Daytona Beach, which went back to 1939, and which had produced most of the umpires who were working through the sixties.

The major leagues selected Ed Doherty to run their program. He had owned the Louisville franchise and had been president of the American Association. The idea was that there would be more time spent in classroom situations, and more time spent in dealing with managers and players. It would also serve as a kind of postgraduate school for the best candidates out of the privately run schools, the most popular being the Al Somers School. Barney Deary was the administrator, and Bill Kinnamon and Joe Linsalata were the supervisors.

There was no charge for tuition, only for room and board, and that point got Al Somers angry. Unfair competition. Al charged tuition, and when the lawyers started getting involved, Major League Baseball gave in on several points.

Barney was a great man. I came to love him like a father. He was a Boston Irishman, about five-ten, medium build, gray hair. He had been in the Marine Corps during World War II, and started umpiring in 1951, working his way up to Triple-A but never crossing over into the big time. Those were, of course, mostly years in which you only had eight games played a day in the majors by the sixteen teams, so they needed only thirty-two umpires, and it was tough to break in. The turnover was always very slow, and a lot of good men never got their chance. I think Barney would have been a good major league umpire, but his turn never came, and he retired in 1965. It was at that time that he got involved in umpire development.

Barney was a very sincere man. You could see it in his eyes. He not only encouraged me when I was still doing Little League in Philly, but he even sent me letters telling me to keep up the good work.

He made me very comfortable at umpire school. It was the first time I had ever been in an almost all-white setting, and he sensed that it could be strange for me. Even though umpire candidates were pretty much rough-and-tumble kinds of guys, for many it was a first-time-away-from-home experience, and when it was necessary to be a father figure, he could be one. In my case, he sensed that I had an even greater burden, and he was always there for me.

Barney was the kind of guy who'd lend you money and let you take plenty of time to pay him back. I know he and his wife would have liked to invite me home for dinner sometimes, but it wouldn't have been right. I couldn't be treated differently from other students. They did have me over after I graduated and was working pro ball, and I always looked forward to spending time with them.

As far as being black, Barney never once suggested that it was going to be a problem for me. "They won't care if you're green," he'd say, and I think as far as he was concerned, he meant it. Whether he was speaking accurately at the time, it was hard to say.

"I fall in love easily," he'd say. "I fall in love with ability. If you work hard, if you show that you've got what it takes, I fall in love with your ability."

And even as we climbed the ladder in the minors and got to the majors, for all of us, he was always back there in Florida as a ready voice to talk to when the going got rough.

St. Petersburg is a great baseball town. It has a tradition that goes back to 1925 when the Yankees started spring training there, with Babe Ruth and Lou Gehrig and those great teams. Later, the Cardinals joined them, and when the Yankees moved to Fort Lauderdale in 1962, the Mets moved in and stayed for twenty-six years. The population of the city is pretty old, but they love their baseball, and they've seen all the great ones pass through.

The weather on the west coast of Florida is usually perfect, and our complex was just fine. We had our dorm, and a lot of fields, with the beautiful green grass and the high, blue Florida sky. It was a perfect baseball setting, and loving the game as much as I did, it was as close to heaven as I'd yet come.

Our routine included morning classroom sessions

followed by lunch. Then we'd split into "teams" with an instructor as the batter, calling out game situations. After dinner we might work on calling balls and strikes off a pitching machine, with a catcher and batter standing in for authenticity.

The classroom sessions were fascinating. I wasn't always that attentive in high school, but here, I saw my future on the line and I knew it was time to pay attention or get out. Bremigan and Kinnamon were the primary classroom instructors, and just as you'd suspect, they'd go over all the rules to their smallest detail, setting up impossible-to-happen situations, just so you'd be ready for anything. And I was a great student. Whereas high school had been a struggle, here I was picking up everything first shot out of the box. It was amazing.

Some guys clowned around but I wasn't there for that. Maybe I had more to lose than they did. I don't know what they were all facing if they failed, but the prospects weren't too bright for me.

We had sixty guys in my class, the Class of '71. Joe Baldino sat next to me in class and became my good buddy. He spent two years in the minors before getting out, and became a successful real estate appraiser in Burbank, California.

I never did memorize the rule book, but I know it as well as anybody. I mean I *know* that sucker. Inside and out. You will never find a manager in baseball who knows it better than I do, and if he tells you he does, he's lying.

You get rated in many ways. Knowledge of the rules is obviously one way. Physical size counts, as does your "presence" on the field. The ability to deal with abuse or to handle disputes is very important. Those things are always going to happen on the playing field.

Timing was an important lesson. Positioning on all possible plays was stressed. The concept of never anticipating a play was hammered into us over and over. And then there was that element of abuse. The question of how well we could take abuse was something we would be measured on, but never tested on beyond a doubt.

In the mock games that we'd play, the instructors would watch us helping out our partners, watching our instincts, watching our reactions, testing us on the rules. And then they'd pick their spots to argue with you and abuse you. The comments were never racial, but they were profane and they were embarrassing.

I'd say, "You mean Mickey Mantle might say something like that to an umpire?" and they'd say, "You bet." It was a revelation.

So they'd attack you and get right in your face and call you terrible names, and they'd see whether you'd run them out of the game and take it. And from that they'd try to determine exactly whether you had what it took. Now understand of course, we knew this was being staged, so obviously, it was a different situation from a real game. That's what I mean about testing you beyond all doubt. Just because you could handle yourself in those mock games over seven weeks in umpire school didn't mean you could hold up under real fire.

Being from the ghetto, I was considered to be in an advantageous spot as far as all of that went. They'd say, "Oh, Eric Gregg, he's from West Philadelphia . . . he's heard everything and seen it all. This guy over here, his father's a minister, he's never gonna believe what he hears." And believe me, no matter how prepared an umpire may think he is after umpire school, it's the on-field abuse that you are never fully prepared for. Some guys just never adjust to it.

I suppose it was true. To this day I've never heard

anything on the field that I didn't hear back home, but I suppose anything's possible, and when someone comes along with something new, I may just tip my cap to him and say, "I salute you—I never heard that before." But it ain't happened yet.

Big John McSherry of the National League was one of my instructors at umpire school. Later, when I got to the majors, we would, on occasion, be on the same crew together.

When John and I were equals, I was like a bird fleeing the nest. He never looked at me as a student, and I never looked at him as a teacher once I'd made it.

Now understand, you can always go to anyone for advice, and that's not considered an act of weakness. But the code of the profession is that you never go to a peer and offer it. You're expected to request it, but not to offer it.

Not to sound like an elder statesman, but today's rookie umpires, when they come into the league, it just doesn't seem that they ask any questions. I always did. For instance, I'd go to McSherry and say, "Hey, Big John, did you notice anything out there today? Do you think I had that call right? Was my timing too quick? How was my judgment? How was my position at third base?"

All of these are the kinds of things that you discuss in umpire school, and should continue to discuss even when you're drawing a paycheck. I don't think you should ever be satisfied and rest on your accomplishments.

Now after a game, you might say "great job" to a partner, but you don't do that every time or it's a meaningless statement. Don't say it if you don't mean it, and don't make a cliché out of it or you'll be wearing it out.

* * *

St. Petersburg did not have a lot of hangouts after hours for a black man. These could be the lonely times for me. I was in the heart of the South, and I'd hear coon jokes when I'd never even heard that word before. I suspect some of those natives said things that made no sense to me and got away with a lot worse.

I couldn't even find a barber who cut a black man's hair. Luckily, I got it cut before I drove south. And since the long Afros were popular then, I grew mine like that and managed to go without a haircut the whole time I was down there.

Baldino was a good buddy, and he even went to the trouble of getting me a fake ID card so I could be twenty-one and go with him to the Playboy Club in Miami.

Big mistake. I'd never been in a place like this before, and my eyes almost popped out of my head. I turned to the first waitress, saw those enormous boobs in the bunny outfit, and immediately knocked her tray of drinks out of her hands by mistake. Oh, what a mess. So everyone started pouncing on me asking for a closer look at that ID, and when I admitted I was only nineteen, we both got thrown out into the street.

The best thing we had turned out to be a little bar called Goofy Port on the Rocks, set up by our own Bill Kinnamon. There were pool tables and pinball machines, and we all went there a lot. There was no James Brown on the jukebox though, mostly Peggy Lee singing "Is That All There Is?", but I'd hang out there with Baldino and the time passed pretty well.

There was another black umpire in the school, an older fellow named Bob Moss, who was a pretty good umpire, but who had taken some bad advice from old Emmett Ashford. Emmett had told him that since they needed black umpires, if he didn't get moved up quickly to Double-A, he should put up a fuss. The problem was, they did have Art Williams moving up at the time, and they didn't go for Moss's bluff. So things didn't work out for him.

Being older, Moss did not really like to hang out with me. He was afraid he'd be denied admission to night spots where they checked IDs carefully. So Baldino was my closest buddy. He made me an honorary Italian, and sometimes jokingly introduced me as "Enrico Gregorio." In my first months after umpire school, when we were assigned to work in "extended spring training games" for minor league players whose leagues hadn't started yet, Deary assigned Baldino, Pallone, and Enrico Gregorio to an umpire squad, and he couldn't wait to call Frank Lucchesi, who was managing the Phillies' farm hands, to tell him the news of his all-Italian umpiring team.

I got along well with the guys in umpire school, and as proof of my acceptance, I was even selected to manage one of the teams we'd divide into when we ran the "championship game." The losing team had to put up all the decorations for our graduation ceremony, and besides my enjoying the honor of being chosen to manage, we won the game.

As school moved on, I was more and more convinced that this was the life for me. I knew my place was on the baseball field. I loved the game. I was smart enough to know I was never going to be a player. But I was realizing that being an umpire not only put me close to the action, it was also making me part of a wonderful world. Baseball was its own universe, far removed from life at The Bottom. I was finding that the friendships I was forming were with people who felt the same way.

I could see a life for myself where I would be running games, where I would be in a position of respect and authority, where my knowledge of the rules and my ability to handle all situations would give me confidence in myself that I might not find in any other profession.

I was feeling a burst of maturity, a rise of the feeling you get when you know that there just isn't anyone who can do it better than you can. Oh yes, that feeling would require a few reminders along the way that experience makes you better, and you don't always know it all, but the feeling was the important thing. I knew that at nineteen, I'd found my niche, and I was determined to make this my life's work.

The instructors seemed to agree. I was rated second in the class when we completed the course. Some instructors probably thought I was still a little young, or I think I might have finished first.

I got a trophy at the graduation ceremonies. It was inscribed, "Most Potential to Go All the Way," and was presented to me by Dallas Green, who was then the assistant farm director for the Phillies. One of my old heroes from the '61 Phillies, who lost those twenty-three straight.

CHAPTER FOUR

Gaining Minor League Experience

THE LITTLE MEMORIES you acquire as you gain experience never leave you. One day, Joe Baldino and I were sitting in the stands at Dodgertown, watching a major league spring training intra-squad game which was being umpired by three older, retired umps. One was Jess Collier, who had been the mayor of Ossining, New York, home of Sing-Sing Prison, and legend had it that he was the guy who would throw the switch in the electric chair. Tough guy to have umpiring. Another was a character named Joe Kane. He told Baldino and me that "players don't really need umpires. They know when they're safe or out. They just need someone to yell it out loud."

Well, he was certainly oversimplifying things to make his point, but he told us to watch him at second base. He worked the entire game with his hands in his pockets, never making a call. On one play, Maury Wills slid into the base. All Kane said was "uh-huh," made no arm motion, and Wills got up and ran to the dugout. It was amazing to see.

Sometime later, Baldino and I were working an intra-squad game in Dodgertown. I remember that Nick Colosi, who'd been a National League umpire for several years, was in the stands observing. Duke Sims, the journeyman catcher who was with the Dodgers then, made a throw to first to pick off Wills. But Maury eluded the tag and we called him safe. Sims argued with Baldino like crazy, even though it was only an intra-squad game. Later Wills told us, "[Wes] Parker didn't tag me, but if that situation ever comes up during a real game, you've got to call the man out. I'm an infielder, and I'd expect that to be an out at second base."

It was a fascinating little exchange. You would never expect a player to give an umpire a lesson like that. I was totally unprepared to ever have a player extend a nice gesture to me. Maury Wills really impressed me. And Parker told Baldino that Sims had no business arguing as much as he did in an intrasquad game. Not long afterward, Sims was gone.

I was hired to be an umpire in the New York–Penn League for the 1971 season. This was one of nineteen minor leagues within professional baseball, formally known as the National Association, with headquarters in Columbus, Ohio.

The New York–Penn League covered a lot of old ballparks and aging facilities, but the climate was comfortable, and the spirits were great on all levels. It was a kick to be part of a first-year league, where everyone dreamed of the big time—the players, the managers, the coaches, the trainers, and of course, the umpires.

My starting salary was $250 a month, plus $250 in expenses. I was young and single, and the money wasn't even important. Whatever it was would have been fine with me. We were assigned partners—each game had two umpires—and whoever served as the driver also got ten cents a mile. That was considered a big deal.

My partner was Josh Madison and we got around in a little Volkswagen Beetle, which I could never even squeeze into today. I learned to drive a stickshift so I could earn some of those dimes per mile they were giving away to the drivers.

The concept of a partner was a new one for me. In umpire school, we were all one big class. Now, it was me and Josh for a season, assigned to work together every game, drive together, stay in the same hotels, share the same locker rooms. It was obvious that we would have to learn to get along well for long stretches, and I'm pleased to say, we handled it just fine. I know that wasn't always the case.

The New York–Penn League, a Class A circuit, was thirty years old, but some of the parks were older, going back to the days when each town was a part of another league. For most of the players in the league, it was a starting off point, with a seventy-game schedule played after the school year ended, intended to get them adjusted up from a thirty-to-forty-game college or high school schedule.

There weren't a lot of big stars in the league in 1971. Jim Rice hit .256 with five homers for Williamsport and the little infielder Mike Cubbage also made the majors. Sixto Lezcano played for Newark, and he later made it big with the Milwaukee Brewers. Batavia had a right-handed pitcher I liked a lot. He was a really decent guy and we hit it off well. He had a 4–3 record with a 4.06 earned run average, and his name was Joe McIlvaine. If that's familiar today, it's because he's now the vice president, baseball operations, for the New York Mets, essentially their general manager just under Frank Cashen. I always enjoy seeing him when I'm at Shea Stadium. But in the New York–Penn League, we all had dreams, and Joe's would have been to pitch in the big leagues. Every day brought the promise of impressing a scout and heading for the big time.

There were usually scouts at the games, particularly since the league, in the Northeast, was in good driving distance to a lot of big league cities. You not only would get the scouts, but sometimes farm directors or general managers. Even as an umpire, you'd sort of pump yourself up a little if you heard a big league GM was in the stands. There was no telling how a good impression might make its way back to the ears of the American or National League offices.

Now, speaking of making an impression, let me tell you about Oneonta, New York, the minor league town closest to Cooperstown (19 miles), and the umpires' dressing room in the duck pond. This was where I made by debut, my very first pro game.

The ballpark, Damaschke Field, is part of a larger municipal park. When I arrived, I asked the first official-looking person I saw, "Where's the umpires' room?"

Cool as anything, he points out to the duck pond beyond the outfield, and says, "Out there."

Sure enough, it was out there with the ducks. Unbelievable. But that's not all.

Now Josh and I are out there suiting up and rubbing up the baseballs when an old guy comes around by the door. Big shot that I am, working my first game ever, I size up the dude as some old-timer from the town who's looking for a free baseball. So I matter-of-factly say, "Josh, give the guy a baseball and send him on his way."

The guy says thanks and takes off. I feel like an old pro, and to tell you the truth, so does Josh, who's no rookie, and was a big, big help in teaching me the ropes. Only this time, we'd both blown it.

So the game begins and Josh and I are wearing our fine new uniforms and there are a couple hundred people in the stands, when, after the top of the first, the public address announcer comes on and says, "Ladies and gentlemen, won't you join us in welcoming a very special guest to Damaschke Field today. We're delighted to welcome an American League supervisor of umpires, Mr. Charlie Berry!"

Oh my god. I look at Josh and he looks back at me, and we immediately realize that we've just thrown the supervisor of umpires out of the duck pond. It was my very first day. I figured we were through.

But Berry was fine. He'd been an American League umpire from 1942 to 1962, and I guess he'd seen everything, including a couple of stupid young umpires throw a guy out of a duck pond. As far as I know, he never held it against us, although Josh never did make it, and I wound up in the National League.

But aside from the duck pond, Oneonta was a pretty neat little city. I stayed in the cleanest little rooming house I ever saw, and they had this Kentucky Fried Chicken place just across the street.

I began to be a connoisseur of the finer dining in the minors. In little Newark, New York—not Newark, New Jersey—they had the best hot dogs in baseball, grilled in green peppers and onions, still the best I've ever had at a ballpark. That's my best memory of Newark.

In Auburn, New York, again there was no locker room for us. The hotel was a real Mickey Mouse one, but that's where we had to dress to go to the ballpark, and people would look at us like we were nuts when we walked through the lobby. We'd come back after the game in those sweaty uniforms and really stink up the place, but then who cared? What sort of folks do you think were staying in a hotel in Auburn, New York, anyway?

Batavia, New York, was one of the strangest cities I ever worked in. For openers, there was no hot water in the locker room, and terrible lighting for the field. Sometimes you'd think you'd better call the game just to save some lives. But the thing I remember most about Batavia was that every night, at exactly 7:45—not 7:44 and not 7:46—there would be an attack of killer bees and killer bugs. You never saw anything like it. One time they almost knocked my hat off. It was as though somebody was keeping these little suckers caged up all day, and letting them go when the alarm sounded at 7:45.

Sometimes I'd be working the plate in Batavia and I'd see on the clock that it was 7:40 and I'd start to sweat. By 7:44, my palms were moist and I was twitching and shaking. Then *bang*, it would be 7:45, and here came the bees. Unbelievable situation. John Kibler, the most punctual umpire I ever worked with, would have loved those bees.

Niagara Falls was also in the league, which gave me a chance to see one of nature's wonders. It was magnificent, but for some reason that year, there was some kind of pollution odor over the whole city, and it was so unbearable, you wouldn't leave your room until it was time to go to the ballpark.

I was selected to umpire the All-Star Game, a really nice first-year honor for me. There was an All-Star party the night before, and Joe Cronin, the American League president, was there with his umpire supervisor Dick Butler. I figured I'd seize the moment and say hi to Cronin, even though I probably shouldn't have even been at the party. I asked Butler to introduce me, but he tried to shoo me away, telling me that Mr. Cronin was busy. He was not very pleased that I was there. So, on my own, I walked over and tapped Joe Cronin on the shoulder and said hello. I know Butler was pretty annoyed at me for doing it, and I don't know how it sat

with Cronin, but that's just the way I was. I'm a friendly
guy, and here was a fellow who might be my boss
someday.

I had a good year. I learned a lot from Josh; I learned
to drive a stick, and I learned to travel by myself and to
live on $250 a month in expense money. When the sea-
son ended, I went back home and worked at the engraving company. I thought I was pretty hot stuff.

It was that winter that I learned that the National
League had purchased my contract, and I was under
their option. After just one year in the minors, I was
now the property of the National League, my destiny in
their hands. You can imagine what a tremendous feeling that was for me. I knew it wasn't an automatic ticket
to the big leagues, but I felt it was a stamp of approval
and that I'd been noticed and been given high grades.
I would still have to improve and prove that I had major
league ability, but for now, it was a very satisfying accomplishment.

With the benefit of hindsight now, I also realize that
it was a time at which the National League was feeling
the pressure to bring a black umpire up, and since there
weren't many to choose from, they jumped at the opportunity to get me before the American League did.
What the signing did in fact was cause some bad feelings between the leagues, and some morale problems
among veteran Triple-A umpires who were working
without options. After I was signed, the leagues got together and agreed on a rule banning the taking out of
an option on a first-year umpire. So I was the last one
who slipped through before that rule.

One immediate result of my being on option by the
National League was that I got to taste the big time during spring training of 1972. I was assigned to work a
game between the Yankees and the Reds in Tampa.

Fred Fleig, my new boss as the National League supervisor of umpires, called me up. He said I'd be working with Shag Crawford, Augie Donatelli, and another minor leaguer, Jerry Smith.

This was another slice of heaven for me. Not only was it a big league game, although spring training, but Crawford and Donatelli were two legends in umpiring. Ever since I began following the umpires, Crawford had been my hero. He had so much style. He was so smooth on the field. I remember one day watching a game on TV. Shag's got third base. A screaming liner goes by him that knocks him off his feet. But cool as anything, from the ground, he makes the foul ball signal, gets up and looks just as stylish as can be.

Anyway, Mr. Fleig tells me I'm working this game, and his parting words of wisdom are, "Eric, just don't screw up." So I said, "Mr. Fleig, I'll do the best I can."

But he answers, "Eric, I don't want you to do the best you can. I just don't want you to screw up."

I guess he had his reservations about a twenty-year-old umpire in a major league setting.

One other thing Fleig said to me was, "You're working home plate."

I was flabbergasted. "Are you sure that's okay?" I asked him. "Don't you think Mr. Crawford or Mr. Donatelli will mind?"

Mr. Fleig said, "Don't worry about it."

So, I arrive at the ballpark: the first one. Shag, my hero, arrives a few minutes later, carefully putting out his cigar before he comes into the little locker room. (The action needed no explanation: We wouldn't be able to breathe if someone smoked in that room). Shag was also a Philadelphia native, having graduated from West Catholic High School. To tell you the truth, I couldn't have been more impressed if Ty Cobb had walked in.

I introduced myself to Shag, and told him that Mr. Fleig told me I should work the plate. I felt a little uncomfortable saying that.

"Oh, is that right?" he said. I half expected him to look for a phone to call Fleig and complain. But he said, "No problem, that's terrific."

Soon Augie Donatelli arrived and he had the same reaction. I later realized how pleased they really were; few veteran umps enjoy doing the balls and strikes on a hot Florida day in spring training. So Augie hands me a couple of boxes of baseballs, and I begin to rub them up with that special mud that's provided in each umpire's room to get the shine off the horsehide. (Today it's cowhide.)

Now, game time is approaching, and I'm beginning to wonder where our fourth umpire, Jerry Smith, is. Like me, he's a rookie. A half hour goes by, and still no Smith.

Suddenly there's a knock on the door. Shag opens it and a beautiful girl is standing there.

"Is Jerry Smith here?" she coos.

"No, I'm sorry, he hasn't arrived yet," says Shag, sounding like a maître d'.

"Oh, well, will you tell him Tammy came by?"

"Sure," said Shag. You could see he was delighted to be taking messages for this tardy rookie.

Finally, Smith arrives. The door pops open and in comes this swaggering fellow smoking a big fat cigar.

"Hey, I'm Jerry Smith," he says. "Any messages for me?"

"I've got one," said Donatelli. "Get the cigar out of the room."

This sets Smith back a little. He changes quietly, goes outside by himself, and doesn't even sit with us.

Jerry Smith was never heard from again. He had the tools, I'm told, to have been a major league umpire. But when you're a Triple-A ump, working your first game, and you make a sour impression on two legends like Shag and Augie, well, I'm not saying that he blew it that day, but it couldn't have helped. And, truth be told, it certainly made me look good. I was polite, respectful, and I called a good game.

I had one tough play at the plate that afternoon. Thurman Munson was heading for home standing up, and Johnny Bench made a swipe tag at him as he sped by. It's one of the toughest calls to make. To tell you the truth, I didn't see whether he actually got him or not, but I threw up my arm and yelled, *"Out!"*

Luck was with me I suppose. Bench did get him, Munson said so when he came behind the plate to catch, and I looked terrific in front of Crawford and Donatelli. After the game, they both told me what a terrific job I'd done. I could have screwed it up and been remembered for blowing it. It could have been all over.

I slept great that night. Just seeing those big league uniforms, working with Shag and Augie, calling a play involving Munson and Bench, it was like it wasn't really happening. But it was.

It was a wonderful experience to get a taste of the majors. I was still very much awe-struck by it. That spring I ran into Al Barlick, a great National League umpire who was elected to the Hall of Fame in 1989. I'd first met him the previous September when I visited Veterans Stadium after the New York–Penn season ended. He asked me where I'd worked the previous season, and said, "How many did you get, kid?" meaning how many people had I thrown out of games in the New York–Penn League.

I answered, "Eight, Mr. Barlick," and he nodded his approval. He said if you're not ejecting people, you're not doing your job right. He told me that some people are *umpires,* but others just carry the title.

Barlick was very much the last of his kind, an umpire who reminded you of the way Bill Klem probably was. Klem was the first umpire to go into the Hall of Fame; a National League umpire from 1905 to 1940, Klem worked eighteen World Series and was credited with the introduction of arm signals. Klem was famous for saying, "I never missed one," and Barlick held that same belief. I don't know any umpire today who makes that kind of a statement, but I know Klem meant "in my heart" when he said he never missed one, and Barlick meant the same thing. Al was also an absolute stickler for perfection. There was no such thing as a "neighborhood play," the so-called automatic out if you're in the neighborhood but missed the base. Barlick enforced those plays, and all plays, to the letter, which is pretty uncommon today.

It was with a lot of pride that I watched him go into the Hall of Fame. I saw the ceremonies on ESPN and again on PRISM cable TV while I was home in Philadelphia. He made a wonderful speech and made me very proud of my profession. He was the sixth umpire to make the Hall of Fame. Besides Klem, there was Tom Connolly, Klem's American League counterpart in terms of longevity; Billy Evans, who later became general manager at Detroit; Cal Hubbard, who's also in the Pro Football Hall of Fame as a player; and Jocko Conlan, a colorful umpire from the 1950s and 1960s.

I had the privilege of working a game involving the Mets that spring, with Willie Mays in the lineup and Yogi Berra managing. Wow! Yogi came to the plate and said something like, "Who rubbed up the baseballs?" and all I could do was stare at him and say to myself, "Wow, Yogi Berra, right here next to me!" I felt like getting his autograph. And Mays, standing just a couple of feet from me. It was awesome.

One day that spring, while Bert Blyleven was pitching for Minnesota, he fired off a curveball the likes of which I'd never seen before. I said to myself, "Man, can I ever call pitches like that one? Am I expected to call this stuff?" It was the first time I'd ever seen a real big league curveball. Oh, did Blyleven ever have one. Still does, I'm told.

The Florida State League, in the familiar surroundings of my umpire school background, was founded in 1919, and often served as a first stop for high draft choices just out of college. It was my assignment for 1972. The league played a long 141-game schedule in the hot summers of Florida, and served as a good test for stamina if nothing else.

In little towns like Cocoa or Pompano Beach, you might play to fewer than five hundred fans a night. Miami and St. Petersburg were the big cities, but even there, attendance was only about fifteen hundred. Sometimes, if you had Max Patkin, the baseball clown, or a special win-a-car night, you might get twenty-five hundred or so. What the small crowds did was make you aware of everything that was going on in the park. By the end of the game, you knew every voice in the stands, every pretty girl's seat location, practically every hot dog vendor's badge number. In short, you were feeling part of a small operation on the low rungs of pro ball. Yet the feeling was exhilarating. Just to suit up and walk onto the field was a joy, each and every day.

We had some older, long-time minor league managers in the league, like Stan Wasiak at Daytona Beach, and Stubby Overmire at Lakeland. Some of the younger managers, like Pete Ward and Russ Nixon, were just starting out, very much like the players and the umps. Early Wynn, the Hall of Fame three-hundred-game

winner, managed Orlando. The most impressive player
in the league was clearly Jim Rice at Winter Haven,
back with me once again. Keith Hernandez was a nine-
teen-year old rookie at St. Pete.

Everyone wanted to win the pennant—that was the
kind of spirit that the players had developed since Little League days. But there was a spirit of advancement
in the air for everyone in the league, much like I'd seen
at the New York-Penn League the year before. That made
for a constant buzz of excitement over achievement on
all levels. We all shared it.

I had some amazing experiences in the Florida State
League. Having gone to school there, I was now pretty
familiar with Florida ways, but I saw some things I hadn't
known about before.

For instance, I met a guy named Papa in Key West,
and he took us to a cock fight. I'd heard about these
things, but I didn't know they really took place in the
U.S. The idea was for two roosters to peck each other
to death, while people around the little ring bet money.
Lots of money.

I wasn't very good about this. In fact, it was so awful, I couldn't stand to look. I actually cried over what
I saw. I didn't know I had that in me, but there I was,
welling up in tears. It was a memorable experience,
something I'll never do again, but it was part of growing up.

It was always nice to umpire in St. Petersburg. Barney Deary and his sweet wife would come to watch me
work, and then they'd take me out to dinner. The field
had just gotten outfitted with Astroturf, which was a new
experience for me. I remember walking around before
the game, bending down and running my fingers through
it, and being amazed at how perfect it was.

St. Pete, as I've said, had a lot of older fans, and

they always had a screen in front of the stands stretch-
ing all the way from first around to third, so that the
older folks wouldn't get hit by even a mild foul ball.

Another good thing about St. Pete was that it was a
Cardinals farm club, and Mr. Busch always saw to it
that there was plenty of cold Bud on hand for the umpires after a game.

You also had a lot of scouts in St. Petersburg, and
as always, you gave it a little extra effort, never knowing when a scout would mention your work to someone
in the league office. In all my years in the minors, I
never knew if any GM or scout ever said one word to
anybody about the umpires, unless they screwed up, but
we always tried a little harder to impress these folks,
just in case. If I had to guess, I'd say that these scouts
could go years without ever seeing anyone from the National League office, but you could always hope.

Even though these were the 1970s, the South was
still the South, and St. Petersburg was very much a
southern city, unlike towns on Florida's east coast, where
more northerners had settled. Racism was still there,
whether you were looking for it or not.

I went with one of my partners, Dallas Parks, to a
white barber shop one day in St. Pete. He was getting
a haircut; I was just along for the company. I sat in a
chair and picked up a magazine while Dallas settled
into the barber's seat for his trim.

The oldest barber in the place, probably the owner,
said to Dallas, "He with you?"

"Yeah," answered Parks, "but he's not getting a
haircut."

"Sorry," said the old barber, "but we can't have that
here. You'll have to ask him to leave."

Geez, Dallas got pissed. If you're kind of neutral
on the race issue—not an activist, just someone passing

through life, not looking for hassles—an incident like that can turn you around. Dallas got out of the chair, said to me, "Let's go," and off we went. He was good to do that, but it was a bad incident for us both. I know Dallas would have liked to belt the guy for what happened, and I was pretty pissed off myself, plus embarrassed.

Anyway, I'd already read all of the magazines the barber had.

Deep down, I might have wanted to hit that guy, but I was now in a situation where I always felt I was being tested. Sometimes you'd see something like that happen and a little voice would say to you, "Is this a setup? Is someone watching this to see if you can handle yourself?" I always felt I had to be a cut above that. And always, I'd control any temper within me and ease out of the situation.

Parks became one of the scab umpires during the strike of 1979, but I never forgot his friendship on the barbershop issue, nor his support. In 1982, he got into a hassle with George Steinbrenner when he threw two Yankees out of a game in two days, and Steinbrenner put out a press release calling him "not a capable umpire." Dallas wound up suing Steinbrenner for libel, but lost the case when a judge in the Bronx ruled that it was just "pure opinion."

Sometime later, I think it was 1973, I was umpiring in the Instructional League in Florida, and we had finished working a game in Bradenton between the Pirates and the White Sox. Mike Flemming, another umpire, said, "Let's go across the street and pick up a six-pack before we head out." It was a little place just across from McKechnie Field. We walked in, and I was the only black there.

The waitress came over to us, smiled and looked at us. She was a nice girl. We were still wearing our umpire uniforms, and had helped ourselves to a six-pack from the refrigerator.

Obviously, this poor little girl had been taught how to deal with these situations.

Polite as can be, she looked us over and said to Mike, "I'm terribly sorry sir, but I'm unable to serve you. I can serve this gentleman [as she pointed to me], but not you folks."

Pretty clever, when I finally figured this all out. So they wouldn't be accused of discriminating against blacks, they simply discriminated against whites in the company of blacks. And they got the expected results. We all had to leave.

Mike got up to go, but I said, "Hey, at least let me finish my beer!" But no good. We were outta there. Right across the street from McKechnie Field, in our umpire uniforms and all. And this was 1973, not 1923.

Over at Lakeland, the manager was Stubby Overmire, just a great guy. Everyone liked him. He was one of those career baseball people, never lacking for a job, never really making a famous name for himself, and certainly never earning much money, but steadily doing his job in the Tiger organization, and making a million friends along the way.

I threw him out of a game one day for arguing a call, and you should have heard people talk about it. It was almost embarrassing to have this on my record. I'd run into other umpires all season and they'd look at me and say, "Eric, you threw Stubby out of a game? You must have really screwed up!"

As I said, Jim Rice was at Winter Haven and he was the talk of the league. He was still growing, but it was obvious that he was going all the way. He knew it too. He said to me one day on the field, "Someday, I'm gonna make a whole lot of money."

Man, was he ever right. The last time I looked it was $2,286,000 a year. Of course back in 1972, no one had any idea that salaries were going to take off like they did. I suspect Rice had $100,000 in mind, which was considered the top figure back then. He was pretty classy, driving around in a '71 Grand Prix, belting doubles and triples and homers, and setting his sights on Fenway Park. He was a good kid. I'm glad he made it.

Over at Tampa, Russ Nixon was the manager, and he later went on to manage in the big leagues. I remember one day when we had to call a game because it was raining like hell, but across the street the sun was shining and it wasn't raining at all. Rainouts just kill the minor league owners, who operate on such a tight budget anyway. It's especially painful when they've already opened the gates, have to pay the ushers and the ticket takers, the ground crew and the cleanup crew, and then you have to refund the tickets to the fans.

With that in mind, you can understand why my biggest blowup of the year had to do with rain in West Palm Beach. They've got a beautiful little ballpark there, very similar to Fort Lauderdale, but like a lot of little Florida sites, they're not that great at getting the field covered. And it can really rain hard sometimes in Florida, very quickly.

This one time, it rained for three days in a row in West Palm, and the management had to call the game each day. I want to tell you, the field was one big mud puddle. I got to the park the fourth day, walking onto the infield before I suited up, and couldn't believe how bad it was.

But the Expos' management had already been hit with three straight washouts, and they were determined not to let it happen again. I couldn't believe it. The field was just unplayable, and unsafe.

But, until the game begins, the decision belongs to the home team. So they opened the gates, filled the seats, sold the hot dogs, and sent the managers out with the lineup cards. I still remember it. Expos against the Cards.

As soon as I got the lineups, I raised my arms up and announced, "I'm calling this game on account of unplayable field conditions." Talk about a gutsy move. The Expos' management went berserk. The general manager called George McDonald, the league president. George spoke to me on the phone, and said, "Eric, I can't believe you did it either, but I'll back you one hundred percent." And he did.

Miami had this old, pre–World War II park. It made you feel like you weren't in beautiful Miami at all, but in some metal army barracks. It was kind of a grimy place, not really loaded up with those nice Florida palm trees and all.

The worst thing about Miami, though, was the general manager, a guy named Red Morcroft. He had been an NFL umpire for twenty-one years, and he had a set of lungs on him you wouldn't believe. And he'd sit in the press box and yell at the umpires. Could you believe it? A former NFL official, yelling at the umps? He made games miserable there for us. Maybe he was trying to impress his friends, but it was really low-class.

The year 1973 found me in the Eastern League, still under National League option, back in the Northeast. I did miss those beautiful little Florida ballparks, but this was Double-A ball. Advancement. Another step up.

Me and Jim Rice, as it turned out. He moved up to

the Eastern League too, going to Bristol. Three straight years of me and Rice, moving up. Jim led the league with a .317 average that year, but he wasn't the talk of the circuit. That was Tom Robson of Pittsfield, who just missed the triple crown, hitting .316 to lose the batting title by a point, but belting 38 homers and driving in 126 runs. It's funny how you could watch two guys in the same league, Rice and Robson, and Robson was clearly the better player. At least to those of us who worked the league. But I guess there was something about him that just fell short of what it took, whereas Rice continued to get better all the time. The real smart scouts could probably have told you that Rice would make it and not Robson. I wasn't so smart. I was pretty impressed by Robson, who went on to play twenty-three major league games for Texas but never hit a home run. He's the Rangers' batting coach today.

Back in umpire school, part of the classroom sessions involved a history of the profession. You've got to know where you've come from to know where you are today.

In baseball's early days, drinking in the stands was common, and the umpires often came in for brutal treatment. In the poem "Casey at the Bat," when the fans yell, "Kill the umpire," that was standard language back then, and while there is no record of any actual killing, drunken fans can get mean, and I have no doubt that stories about soda bottles getting chucked out at the umps were real. One of the reasons most parks sell cups of soda now instead of bottles is the "kill the umpire" mentality some people still might get after too much beer.

Waterbury, Connecticut, was an old blue collar town, and you could almost imagine "Casey at the Bat" having taken place there. The Dodgers ran the club, and they had a poor choice as manager, Don "Ducky" LeJohn, who had played a little for them in Los Angeles before becoming a minor league manager.

LeJohn played the crowd, and he had a way of getting the fans mad at you. That wasn't good. One day he pulled that when I was there, and sure enough, when I left the park that night, I was pelted by cups and ice. It was a nasty situation, but I had the presence of mind to just keep going and get out of there. Still, I couldn't help but picture the umpires of the turn of the century, back in baseball's roughest days, sneaking out of town under cover of darkness to avoid the lynch-mob fans of the time.

I'll tell you what I loved in the Eastern League— my first taste of Canada. I came to like all Canadian cities. They were the best towns in the minors. You were always treated so well; the girls were so friendly, and white people seemed to like black people more. They were less suspicious of them, more eager to be friends.

I also learned a little French as part of the experience. It seemed the first thing you'd learn was how to start a conversation with a girl. Later on you'd learn how to order off a menu. But the words you'd use to meet girls were the top priority.

Doug Flynn was a classy little infielder who played for Three Rivers that year, or "Trois Rivers" as the natives called it. Doug and I both agreed that the Canadian cities were great. Years later when we were both in the National League, we'd still laugh about the Eastern League towns, and talk about how much we looked forward to going to Montreal.

My other big memory of that season was at Reading, Pennsylvania, during the playoffs. I remember Dallas Green, the Phillies' farm director, sitting behind me in the stands. Reading had John Stearns, the catcher who later played for the Mets. Here comes Stearns now, playoff situation against Pittsfield, and he calls time, steps out, looks me right in the eye and says, "I'm gonna hit one out now."

Just like that.

"You cocky little SOB," I said to myself. "Get in there" was all I said to him.

And don't you think he belts one out on the very next pitch? I'll never forget it. I was in such shock that I couldn't even say anything when he came across home plate. I mean, I was in awe. I never umped a game again with Stearns in it that I didn't think of that.

After the season, I went back home to the engraving job in Philadelphia. One day the telephone rang at my mother's house, and she took the message—*call Barney Deary.*

I called him back from work. (I must owe the engraving company a lot of money in phone calls.)

"Eric," he said, "an opportunity has opened up in the Dominican Republic I want to talk to you about. There are three umpires who just got fired there, and it's the middle of their season."

"Why did they get fired, Mr. Deary?" I asked.

"Well, never mind about that for now," he said. "They need three replacements in a hurry, and I've recommended you, Steve Palermo, and Rich Garcia. I think it's a great opportunity for you to keep working, improve your skills, and uh, deal with new situations."

"What kind of situations?"

"Well, it's a little different down there, but the rules are the same and this would be a chance for you to get some more work in."

Sure, I figured, there was something fishy about it,

but Barney was a straight shooter, and if it was dangerous or something, he wouldn't have called me. So I
agreed to go. I felt like Clint Eastwood, heading off to
clean up a bad situation.

Baseball, as played in the Dominican Republic, finds
the fans very involved in the games. The stands were
about half and half, black and white, and the people
would drink rum and Coke all day. They were very vo-
cal and very into the game, even more so than in New
York. Occasionally you'd hear gunfire go off during a
ball game, but it was only the police trying to quiet a
situation by firing in the air.

You might get ten to fifteen thousand fans for the
games, especially when the two big rivals, Licey and
Escogido, played. The parks were old but well kept,
and I remember how one of the traditions would be that
they'd play the two national anthems—the Dominican
and the U.S.—and all the activity in the stands would
come to a halt as the fans rose in silence. That would
be the cue for kids to climb over fences and gates and
sneak into the park. With everyone standing, it was easy
for them to mix into the crowd, and the police wouldn't
chase them during the anthems, so it was a routine the
kids carried out every day.

It was a great opportunity for me. Most Latin stars
play ball there during the winter months, and they're
heroes in their home countries. And there were a lot of
big league stars there. Rico Carty was one, J. R. Richard, Joaquin Andujar, Steve Garvey, Steve Yeager, and
my all-time pitching hero, the great Juan Marichal. His
career was pretty much nearing a close, but he was a
legend in the Dominican Republic, and it was expected
that the local stars would play.

My first game was Marichal against Andujar. The
past against the future. Great matchup, great game. In

fact, the whole season was a great experience. Barney was right. There were no problems, and I had a wonderful time. I liked the people, and loved staying active. I told him to see if he could get me down there the following winter. Now *that* one would be interesting.

I was moved up to the Pacific Coast League for the 1974 season. This was a big promotion, one I had counted on all during my year in the Eastern League. The PCL could be the last stop, or it could be the big break. It was a first class, Triple-A league, and many umpires went to the majors from there. The pay was $750 a month and finally, we got free hotel and airfare included. Also, it was a league with a lot of great stops, including Hawaii, and although I'd be far from home, I was a big boy now, and that didn't bother me a drop. I'd grown up a lot since I walked out of West Philly High and marched off to umpire school. I was still only twenty-three, but you gain a lot of maturity and a lot of wisdom on the road.

Even when I'd get home, my folks would say, "Hub, how come you're talkin' so genteel . . . you sound like a white man!"

I laughed. They were partly right. I was living as a lone black man in a very white world, and I was picking up a lot of their speech patterns and habits. They were picking up some of mine too, but it was happening to me more than to them.

I would spend four years in the PCL, and I knew it like the back of my hand by the time I was through with it. And of course, it was not without its special memories and adventures.

Take Hawaii, for instance. Awesome place. Just beautiful. The way they would work it would be that you'd go there twice a season, usually for two weeks, but my very first time there was a three-week stay, which is longer than I'd ever been assigned to one place at a time. You could actually unpack, put things on hangers, and pretend you were living there.

I had my worst nightmare in Hawaii though. An out-and-out, unprovoked brawl on the beach, with me as the unsuspecting and pummeled loser.

It was on my final trip there, after the playoffs. I was lounging on the beach, sucking up the sun about four o'clock one afternoon when a little Samoan kid comes by.

Friendly as I always am to people, I said, "How ya doin', kid, what's your name?"

He turned and ran away as fast as he could. Could be I scared him I suppose. I was over two hundred pounds, a big black guy sitting out on the beach, and he's this little kid in a strange place. I understand these things.

But now he comes back, looks me right in the eye and says, "My dad says don't talk to me."

I guess I gave him a puzzled look, but hey, no big deal.

Suddenly, here comes his father.

"You got a problem?" he says.

I said, "What are you talking about? I just said hello to your kid!"

"Well, leave my kid alone," he shouts, so I wouldn't mistake his words over the sounds of the waves.

And the next thing I know, this guy's on top of me, just kicking the shit out of me. Unbelievable! He's belting me with closed fists, pounding me into the sand; I was completely unprepared and helpless. Finally I wriggled away and threw my beach chair at him. I start screaming at him, but he's a crazed animal. He picks me up now, throws me down into the sand and says, "Have you had enough?"

Well, now my umpire partners come running over. They were a little further down the beach and not close enough to help out right away.

Here come Ed Montague and Bill Lawson, like the cavalry to the rescue, and we have an old-fashioned western brawl, right there on the sand, with a crowd starting to form around us. I get up, pretty bloody now, and, out of breath, say, "Okay, I've had enough."

But he floored me again, or sanded me, I suppose I should say.

People started to cheer for me like I'd been winning. This is just getting the big Samoan guy even madder. So he looks at me and says, "You didn't win, nigger."

"Nigger?" I yelled. "Nigger? Your nose is bigger than mine!" With that, everyone who was watching started to laugh. They thought it was a pretty funny line, but the Samoan guy only got angrier hearing the laughter. He was on fire.

With that, I grabbed a souvenir toy spear from one of the "spectators," and started charging the guy like some Zulu warrior. Now here come the cops.

Montague tells me to drop the spear, which probably was an eighty-nine-cent toy anyway, and says, "Don't press charges."

"Don't press charges?" I think to myself. I've seen enough of these things in the movies. I'm picturing myself getting hauled off to jail for saying hello to the little kid.

My eyes were swollen, my nose was broken, and I was bleeding into the sand. I guess the cops could tell that I was the loser, not the criminal, and they just dispersed the crowd and broke things up.

Someone told me later that Samoans just hate

Americans because we take their women or something. I don't know, but he sure was pissed at me.

The only good thing to come out of it was I got a nice Seiko watch, which fell out of his pocket during the brawl. I was continuing the Gregg tradition, like my grandfather who got all of those watches over the years.

It seemed like they always had rain in Spokane, but, this being a Triple-A league, eventually they had to get all the games played, one way or another. So they tended to play under tough conditions, because they never knew when they could make up games. I mean, it's not easy flying the Hawaii team back for a makeup game.

This particular series was the final one of the year. It was the next-to-last day of the season, September 6. It had rained nonstop for two days and the field was drenched, but it was important to get the game in and get the gate in, and Bill Cutler, the GM of Spokane, hired a crew to spill gasoline on the field. They set the gas on fire to dry out the place, and then they flew over with a helicopter to get the smoke cleared out. I'm telling you, this was some amazing thing to see. What a production; it had to be more entertaining than the ball game. I'm sure it was expensive, but I suppose it was worth it to get the game played. It was a very elaborate operation.

Well, they completed their operation, they sold their fifteen hundred tickets, got the crowd seated, had the national anthem, the exchange of lineups, we went over the ground rules, and it was time to play ball. I'm working home plate. We play two innings. No problem.

Sal Butera is catching now for Tacoma in the bottom of the second. Suddenly, I become aware of the smell of gas. It was the gas they used to dry the field. And it's starting to make me dizzy.

I call time and walk around a little to clear my head. Butera smells it too, and he's also walking around. The fans have no idea what's going on.

We both put on our masks and try again. No good. I said, "Sal, I can't do it." Rob Ellis, the Spokane catcher, had smelled it too.

I called the other umpires over. They're also smelling it. They can take it a little better, but at home plate, it was the worst. So I raise my arms, wave the teams off the field, and call time. I give the ground crew about a half hour to get rid of the fumes, but they just can't do it. John Felske, managing Spokane, was sympathetic, and admitted that he was getting a headache, even in the dugout. Finally, I had to call the game off.

Oh, Cutler just went off the wall. All the expense to dry the field, and all for nothing. He couldn't believe it. You never saw a GM so mad. Truth was, I could hardly blame him. I would have been just as mad. But I had to do what I had to do. What a scene. The poor fans had no idea what it was all about.

Roy Jackson, the league president, backed me up completely, which probably took some guts, because he wasn't there and couldn't appreciate the smell. But I told him straight, and he backed me all the way. I still think of this one as the "Gasout Game."

Frank Howard was the manager of Spokane in 1976, the only minor league managing job the big guy ever had. He was a very intense person, besides being enormous. He was also the only person who ever came looking for me in the locker room to argue about a play on the field.

It was over a bang-bang play at the plate against Tacoma. Rick Renick was on second for Tacoma when Al Woods hit a sharp single to right. Now you've got a one-bounce throw to Rob Ellis, the catcher. There was a head-first slide, a lot of dust, I waited for it to clear, and called it "safe." It was the game-winning run.

Oh, what an argument we had. Howard and Ellis were going nuts. Since the game was over, the threat of the fans spilling onto the field and joining in was present. In fact, when other Spokane players started surrounding me, they called security guards onto the field to escort us to our locker room.

When the game ended, Howard showed up at our locker room. He stood there naked except for a towel around his waist. He had several players behind him. He was smoking a cigar, and he was a formidable sight, all six feet eight inches of him. And he was still mad as hell, and looking for blood. I don't think he was drunk, but I reached for my mask and put it on to protect myself, just in case. What a sight. He started shaking his finger at me and yelling something like, "Don't you ever screw with my kids again."

He got suspended for the rest of the season, although there were only two games left. Wherever Howard coaches these days, I always read about what a good guy he is, but I'll never forget the sight of him at our locker room door.

Sacramento was a strange stop in 1974. Bob Lemon, a great guy, was their manager, and they played in this crazy little ballpark with Mickey Mouse dimensions. The Sacramento Solons hit 305 home runs for the season, probably an all-time minor league record. Lemon used to joke that he had to wear a golf glove just to be able to shake hands with the guys when they homered.

Their big bashers were Bill McNulty with fifty-five and Gorman Thomas with fifty-one. It was a joke to work games in that ballpark that season, but it was pretty amazing to be there and watch baseball history being made. The fans loved it. Even though the team finished in last place, they led the league in attendance.

The Arizona cities, Phoenix and Tucson, were strange places to me because of that weird desert heat. We would play day games in 118 degrees. You'd be sweating to death in the first inning and then be all dry in the second. It was like a sauna effect.

Tucson also got my award for having the worst and ugliest mascot I ever saw, some lunatic in a bull suit known as the Tucson Toro. How he ever got his head into that suit I'll never know.

Salt Lake City was fascinating. This was Mormon country of course, and you just assumed that everyone you met there was a Mormon. Well I want to tell you something about Mormons in ballparks. Those fans cursed the umpires worse than any fans anywhere. It was a brown bag town—they'd bring their own booze in brown bags to the park, drinking and swearing like you couldn't believe. And it was a small park too, so they were right on top of you.

I suppose if you confronted them about it later, they'd say, "Oh, those weren't Mormons cursing at you; Mormons don't curse. They were probably fans from the visiting team, or other cities."

Yeah, right.

I'm pretty sure I spent an extra year in the minors as a result of having two protests upheld in games I umpired in 1975. At least John McSherry convinced me that was the case.

Bill Lawson, my partner, was sometimes a little shaky in tight situations, but when a protest is upheld, it's a real embarrassment to the league, and reflects upon both of the umpires working the game. And for two in one year to go against us certainly looked bad.

The first one, at Tacoma, involved a suspended game due to rain that was resumed the next day. It was the top of the fifth inning, and there was some question as to who the hitter was supposed to be. The official scorer told us it was Sonny Jackson, the old Atlanta Braves infielder, now playing for Hawaii. He bats and gets on base. Now Cal Ermer, managing Tacoma, comes out to protest that Jackson was the wrong hitter.

"Cal," we say, "your own official scorer told us it was Jackson."

He argued, but we let Jackson stay at first. So he filed a protest, and damned if he didn't win it. Lawson and I felt this was wrong, because it was the Tacoma official scorer who said it was Jackson, but we lost it, and the game had to be replayed. It didn't look good on our records.

Some weeks later, we had the same teams, Hawaii and Tacoma. Ermer came out to argue that the Hawaii pitcher was loading up the ball.

Lawson went to the mound to check the pitcher, and said he found a substance on the pitcher's cap, probably Vaseline.

I said, "Bill, we've got to throw him out." But Bill said, "No, you just don't do that—guys never get thrown out for this," and we let him stay. Ermer protested again, so Lawson had to write up a report. And in the report, he said that upon inspection, he had discovered a "sticky substance" on the cap.

If he'd just said substance, we would have survived the protest. But he used the word sticky, and the league had to agree with the protest, and make the teams play again. So that was two strikes against us in one season, and I'm convinced to this day that it cost me an extra year in the minors.

CHAPTER FIVE
Conchita

I LOOKED FORWARD to returning to the Dominican Republic after the 1974 season. I'd had a good experience there in '73, even learned a little Spanish, and hey, the winter was nicer than in Philly.

Also, I felt I was closing in on the majors, and the added experience would help me, as well as impress the National League office.

Experience is what separates the good umps from the pack. You have to have those seasons under your belt to be ready to face anything that might come up. Your attitude on the field matures. You call plays a little slower, you feel less pressure to make the quick call. You learn how to calm people down better. Let them have their say; sooner or later they start repeating themselves, and then the conversation, or the argument, has nowhere else to go. The more you're around, the calmer you get. Even dealing with screaming managers requires seasoning. You might think you have just the right temperament for it, but then along comes some guy who makes you realize you haven't seen it all just yet. Tommy Lasorda would be a good example.

Lasorda and I go back to the Dominican Republic

days, when he was still a Dodger coach and I was still a Triple-A umpire. So we've got a history: over fifteen years of working together. Some of it's been great; all of it's been memorable and some of those memories were written in the Dominican.

I had a Dominican girlfriend in '74. She was a very pretty girl, and she was patient with my language problem.

We had a new umpire with us that year, a fellow named Bill Rosenberry. I asked my girlfriend if she had a friend for Bill, so that we might double-date.

Funny thing down there was that they didn't have many telephones, and if you wanted to get a message to someone, like I was doing to set up the double date, you had to hire a cab driver to deliver the message. It was a dime if he went in a straight line, and an extra dime for every turn he had to make. The system worked.

My girlfriend did have a friend, a white girl named Ramona Camilo, nicknamed Conchita. It was all set. And the four of us went out on October 18, 1974.

Well, the two girls met us in a cab. We're standing there, and out they come. First my girl, then Conchita, who was wearing tight jeans with high heels and a long-sleeved shirt tied up at the waist. I took one look and said, "Billy, you're taking my girl; I've got Conchita."

Just like that.

To say we hit it off fast is an understatement. It was one of the fastest courtships on record. I was so comfortable with her. She told me that she liked how aggressive I was; how even though I made so many mistakes in trying to speak Spanish, I was never embarrassed to keep trying.

"I make plenty of mistakes in English too," I told her.

I was falling deeper in love by the minute. We went back to my hotel to go swimming in the pool. I started to make my usual moves on her, telling her how beautiful she looked in a bathing suit. She told me she thought I was cute.

I said, "Conchita, come to my room: I want to show you my equipment."

She laughed and blushed and shook her head. Then I laughed too. "No," I said, "I mean my umpire equipment!"

So she came upstairs and I let her try on all the umpire gear and then there was a knock on the door.

It was her sister, Isolda, whom I had met before. She didn't know a word of English. I think she was amazed to find such an innocent but silly-looking scene.

Conchita's grandmother passed just as the holidays were approaching that winter. As was the custom, Conchita wore black every day. She was very religious. At one point during this mourning period, she asked me if I'd like to meet her mother.

We went by their home, her mother spoke, and Conchita translated as best as she could.

"My mother says that if you really love me you'll marry me," she said.

"Your mother said what?"

I was stunned. It had never passed my mind. But it made me stop and think. I was crazy about Conchita, and I'd been on the road, umpiring for four years. It's hard to meet good women in that kind of life. Even though I was only twenty-three, it could be a good thing for me, settle me down, give me some roots.

I told Conchita I would think about that one.

Needless to say, it was all that was on my mind for the next few days. I mentioned it to Rosenberry and he said, "Are you outa your mind?"

I think Conchita's family figured I was in the black mafia or something. An important man. A lot of people in the Dominican Republic had taken to calling me Diablo—the devil. There was something about being as big as I was and as black as I was, especially in a country that was very religious, but also one that toyed around with mysticism and voodoo. That was more to be found in Haiti, but they had it there too.

I had one more thing I needed to do.

Call Barney Deary back in St. Petersburg.

He was happy to hear from me, but immediately figured there was some problem on the umpiring scene.

"No, Mr. Deary," I said, "nothing like that at all. It's this girl I met here . . ."

"Are you in trouble Eric? Did you get her in trouble?"

"No, nothing like that either. I love this girl. I'm absolutely crazy about her. I'm probably gonna marry her. But I needed to ask your opinion on something, and I'll tell you right up front, your answer might not even matter, but I wanted to hear what you say anyway."

Barney waited.

"Well, the girl is white. And I was just curious as to what you thought this would mean in the National League office. I mean, you know how they think; will this keep me from being a big league umpire?"

There was a pause. Then Barney said, "Eric, you love the girl? My advice is marry her."

That was it. It was what I wanted to hear. Barney knew that. Did he think that it would have a bad effect on my getting promoted? I never knew what he really felt, but I knew Barney Deary well enough to know that he told you things straight. And it was good enough for me.

I went to see Conchita.

"Let's do it honey," I said. "But it's going to be my wedding; I'm paying for it, and we'll make a great party out of it on New Year's Eve. Only thing is, I want your mother to send me over two nice pigs for roasting."

It was part of the local custom.

I called home to let my mother know my plans. Mostly, she just wanted to know if Conchita was pretty. She was all for it. My father was another story. He was dead set against it, mostly because she was white, and he was uncomfortable with that.

Unfortunately, none of my family could afford to come down for the wedding, and it was pretty short notice too, but that was understandable.

Well, New Year's Eve came, December 31, 1974, ten weeks after we'd met, and everything was set. I invited all the other umpires, all my friends, and got a band. We got married at five o'clock in the afternoon and then started to party.

The two pigs arrived in a big cardboard box, and we got right to roasting them and had a great time.

The only snag that occurred was that the local hotel was completely sold out, and we had no car to get to another one. So we borrowed a motorcycle and drove forty-five minutes to a different hotel, Conchita on the back, and me up front with the remains of the second pig on my shoulder. We ate the rest of it that night in the hotel.

I was a crew chief that season, and since there weren't many teams in the league, I was doing Tom Lasorda's games a lot of the time. And even though he was still just third base coach for the Dodgers, he was a big man in the Dominican Republic. Let's face it, Tommy just has this way about him. People think he's important, and he loves the spotlight. Even when he was just a coach, he had Frank Sinatra as a buddy, promising to sing the national anthem when he became manager.

Anyway, Tommy could get anything done. He always knew the right people. You know those electric eye doors that open when you approach? Doors opened for Tom even before those things were invented. And now I had a new wife and I needed a visa for her to return to the U.S. with me. With the red tape down there, such a thing could take months. So I went to Lasorda and asked if he could help me get a visa for Conchita.

"No problem," he said. And bang, we had one in a couple of days.

The next season, I was back again, and so was Tom. He didn't have such a good team this time around and the wins were few and far between. He was trying to do well so that he would get the Dodger managing job when Walt Alston retired. And his patience was running a little thin.

One day, he had a guy trying to steal home, and I called him out. Those plays are almost always arguments, because they're almost always close, you've got a tangle of bodies and equipment, and the view from the dugout is usually bad. I'm convinced they were plays invented just to get umpires in trouble.

Anyway, Lasorda's guy was out at the plate. And Tom was furious. He was out there screaming and screaming and finally he said, "And after I did you that big favor last year!"

I said, "You mean the visa? Tom, that has nothing to do with this."

And he stormed off.

But this wasn't over.

The next day, Bobby Valentine, one of the Dodgers' top prospects, was up for Lasorda's team. I was umpiring at third, and suddenly, Valentine fires his bat clean over my head. I know that was partly Tom's doing, and I threw Valentine out of the game.

Bobby was hopping mad. Things were getting tense, and in the argument, that big Rico Carty comes after me and calls me a dummy.

Carty, he was just no good. Never liked him. So I look at him and I say, "Are you calling *me* a dummy? You're gone too."

I have to admit, to run Carty took some nerve. He was like a god down there to those fans.

By now, Carty's just as crazy as Valentine and he gets right up to my face and says, "You're a nigger." I back away, look at him in disbelief, and say, "Rico, you're blacker than I am!"

"Don't matter," he answers, "I'm Spanish."

Well, the place is going crazy now. And here comes Lasorda at last.

"You stuck it to me last night," he said, "and now, this. You throw out two of my guys! You stupid . . ."

He hesitated for just a second. I had seen that look before and I knew what was coming.

He said his piece and jumped up and down and he had the crowd out of control now.

This was an awful mess. Not only had he gone too far in arguing with me, but he was inciting the fans after I'd thrown Carty out. It was getting scary.

It was tempting to shoot back at him, but I remembered my training and resisted stooping to that level. This was the real test of an umpire. So I controlled myself, and finally, he just walked off.

But by now, things were out of control. All sorts of things were being thrown out onto the field at me, and

I'm thinking that I've still got to go through Lasorda's dugout to get to the protection of our little locker room.

I got hit by some whole oranges, and the place was in an uproar. Somehow we restored order and I escaped with my life.

I went back to the hotel and called Barney. I was thinking, "He got me into this mess in the first place." I wanted Lasorda suspended; maybe even Carty and Valentine. I was hopping mad myself.

But the league office there doesn't have such power. The owners run the league, and there was no way that they'd get any of their players or managers suspended. It was a bad situation. I was beginning to see how I got hired in the first place, and what had happened to the three umpires who got fired to create the openings.

So my partners supported me and we went on strike, demanding suspensions. Games were canceled, and we waited three or four days to see if Lasorda was going to be disciplined.

We lost. We all got fired. They simply hauled three more umpires down and resumed play. I was out of a job.

It was unbelievable. I wondered if it would spoil my career in the States, but Barney told me I had done the right thing, and that I took a position that would be respected in the league office.

My partners went home, but I stayed the rest of the winter since Conchita was with me and it was her home.

I want to say that the Tom Lasorda who pulled that in the Dominican Republic is not the same Tom Lasorda I work with today. He would never pull that stuff in the States. He knows better.

To excuse Valentine a little, and maybe Lasorda too, people just act differently when they're away from home. It's as though no one's looking, so anything goes. I mean,

Valentine would never throw a bat like that in the States. I think being away from home brings out a lot of personality traits in people they didn't even know were there.

Of course, even the natives act differently down there. Pedro Borbon, the fine Cincinnati pitcher, was a big hero in the Dominican Republic. But he'd think nothing of calling time out, running into the stands to beat some poor guy up who'd been getting on him, then going back to the mound to continue the game.

A couple of years later, Lasorda was a rookie manager in the National League and I was a rookie umpire. In my first series with him, at the Astrodome, I ejected him three days in a row.

So I got a phone call from Fred Fleig in the league office, and he said he wants to see me when I'm in New York.

I went up there, he looked me in the eye and said, "Do you have a grudge against the Dodgers?"

A yes answer, of course, could mean the end of my career. At least I was that smart. And besides, I had no grudge against the Dodgers at all, which is what I told him.

"How about Lasorda?" he asked.

"You mean because he almost got me killed in the Dominican Republic a couple of years ago?" I answered. "No sir, I've forgotten all about that, Mr. Fleig." "That's fine," he said. "That's all I wanted to know." And the meeting was over. Lasorda and I get along fine now, and I actually like the guy, in his own way. Sometimes now he'll come running out to argue a play, and I'm wondering, "What's going on here," and he'll say, "Eric, we're on national TV, I just need a little camera time."

As for the Dominican incident, it's history. Naturally, you don't forget something like that, and he never has apologized, but I'm big enough to say, "Let's move on with our lives." That was long ago and far away.

You do get incidents like the Carty thing on occasion in the U.S., but they're few and far between. There was this big slugger in the Pacific Coast League, Craig Kusick, and he came running out screaming at me one day and his face tightened and he said, "You . . . you . . . big . . ." He couldn't seem to get it out.

So I said, "Go ahead, Craig, I've heard it before."

So he finishes the sentence, and I say, "Feel better?" Then boom, I ran him.

One day in Atlanta, this fan was sitting behind home plate, where I'm working, and he yells to me, "Boy, I've got this big watermelon, and every time you miss a pitch, I'm gonna take a bite."

I had to laugh. As the game goes on, he keeps telling me how little watermelon is left.

After the 1975 season in the Coast League, I stayed behind in Tucson for a while with Conchita and another umpire, Dick Adams.

Dick gave up umpiring shortly afterwards when he thought he had cancer. But it turned out he didn't have it. He's now the mayor of Taylorville, Illinois.

Anyway, I got a phone call from Fred Fleig when Dick was with me. Conchita was out shopping.

"What are you doing on September 26th?" he asked.

"No plans, Mr. Fleig," I said. "Do you need me for a meeting in New York or something?"

"No, not exactly," he answered. "I need you in Cincinnati. Lee Weyer's the crew chief. I want you to work the last couple of weeks of the season."

That was the *National League* season he was talking about.

This did not mean I had made the majors. This was not an uncommon thing. It was a chance to give young umpires a look at the big time. But for me, it was the call of a lifetime.

Conchita came back and I had this big smile on my face. She wanted to know what was going on, and I jumped up and down with the excitement of the news. She was thrilled too, even though I told her I couldn't take her with me.

When I got to Riverfront Stadium in Cincinnati, I was amazed by how classy everything seemed, how well organized big league ball was. First, there was a five-thousand-dollar check waiting for me to cover my salary and expenses for the rest of the season. My own locker was right there with my name above it. I had new equipment and a new pair of Adidas shoes. I was measured for a new uniform.

This was all too much to believe. Complimentary Bloody Marys on the flight—I ordered seconds—and first class travel.

When I went to home plate for the exchange of lineups, I shook hands with Sparky Anderson of the Reds and Connie Ryan of the Braves, the managers. I looked into the Reds' dugout. There were Pete Rose, Johnny Bench, Joe Morgan, Tony Perez, Dave Concepcion, George Foster, Ken Griffey, all the "Big Red Machine" guys. Guys I'd been watching on TV just the week before.

Right after the lineup exchange, the Reds took the field. The public address announcer asked everyone to stand for the national anthem.

Cincinnati's a respectful town. There wasn't a sound during the anthem. But I was standing there looking at the flag, my chest out, my stomach in, and a grin from ear to ear. Satch Davidson, standing next to me, said, "Kid, what are you gonna do now?"

I answered, "As soon as the music's over, I'm gonna let out a scream just as loud as I can."

The music ended, the fans started cheering, and I let out a war whoop like you've never heard. My three partners all broke up. They understood. They'd all had their first games in the big leagues.

What they hadn't had was a journey from The Bottom to the top. I was the third black umpire in big league history. Art Williams was still in the league; Emmett Ashford was retired. I hustled out to third base and stood there just basking in it all, letting the moment last forever.

Between innings, about midway through the game, Lee Weyer, the crew chief, called me down from third.

"What did you think of that pitch I just called on Bench?" he asked.

It was one of those borderline low strikes we sometimes call *shinburgers.*

I said, "Hey, that was right there! Great call!"

Weyer laughed. He was just playing with me. He knew I'd say that. But I went along with it. It was all part of the trip.

I remembered Fred Fleig's advice, or instruction, when I did the major league spring training game. "Eric," came the voice from the past, "just don't screw up."

I didn't. I had a great series. I did terrific. Go ahead, ask me.

CHAPTER SIX

Weighing into the Majors

IN 1976 AND 1977 I made a few more guest appearances in National League ballparks, mostly filling in for sick umpires. But in 1978 I was called up for good—I had finally made it all the way.

I wasn't the only rookie on the umpiring scene in 1978.

A persuasive attorney named Richie Phillips, who by coincidence was also from Philadelphia, was chosen at the beginning of the year to represent the umpires' union. He took the place of John Cifelli, and argued that the contract Cifelli had negotiated was not binding, as the umpires had never given Cifelli power of attorney.

Richie Phillips had done great things with the NBA officials, and there was a climate of improved working conditions throughout baseball in the late 1970s which began with the Players Association winning free agency under their lawyer, Marvin Miller. Phillips didn't come cheaply, but a lot of guys, particularly Bruce Froemming, Paul Runge, Jim Evans, Terry Tata, Joe Brinkman, and Larry Barnett were very high on him. Richie felt more could be done for the umpires, and set out to give us a stronger and more effective union. Previous attempts at such a thing didn't accomplish very much. As recently as 1968, two American League umpires, Al Salerno and Bill Valentine, were dismissed by Joe Cronin, presumably for trying to organize a union. This resulted in a grievance before the National Labor Relations Board, the first time baseball had ever been called before them, and in the end, while Salerno and Valentine didn't get their jobs back, the union came to be accepted. Augie Donatelli was a big man in getting it activated.

Now of course for me, I was just so happy to be there that I practically would have paid them just to be standing on those beautiful major league fields. But you can't let that enthusiasm get in the way of the fact that this was to be my career, my means of support for my family, and perhaps the beginning of a thirty- to forty-year association with baseball. It made sense for me to listen, and to look after my future, as well as the futures of my fellow umpires.

I have to admit that I was pretty surprised when we went on strike on August 25. But Richie had shown us, step by step, item by item, that the agreement we were working under was simply not in our best interest.

Hotel costs, for example, were killing us. We usually had to dig into our own pockets to pay our travel expenses, which was just plain unfair. We were getting fifty-two dollars a day to cover hotel rooms, in-town transportation, and three meals. The contract, which was to run through 1981, included only a one-dollar-a-day increase in that allowance yearly.

I was in Atlanta on the day of the strike, and I have to admit I sat there saying, "Can this be happening?" There was no way I was going to go against the union or my fellow umpires, but when you're a rookie and everything is going so well, you wonder how the timing came out like this. I'm sure it was the same kind of feeling that Fernando Valenzuela had during his spectacular rookie season of 1981, when all of a sudden the Players Association went out.

The strike only lasted one day. The league presidents, Chub Feeney and Lee MacPhail, got a court order forcing us back to work the next day. But it was a tuneup for the following year: a warning to the leagues that Richie Phillips meant business, and a warning to the umpires that a strike was something that could happen.

My weight problem increased the higher I went in pro ball. The more cheeseburgers and beer I could afford, the more I ate. I didn't seem to be learning much about balanced diets and cholesterol levels and things like that. When you're working all those minor league towns, eating on the run, and just trying to get filled up on good food, you develop bad eating habits and an expanding waistline.

When I started in umpire school, I had lost nearly sixty pounds to get down to 180. At seventeen, as Hub to everyone at West Philadelphia High School, I was a mean 240. But in 1978, my rookie year in the majors, I was 205, which didn't look bad at all on a 6'3" frame. Still, I began to gain weight as the year went on and big league food was in front of me. No wonder my fifty-two dollars didn't go very far.

I guess I made one of my worst predictions ever when I did a newspaper interview in the Pacific Coast League. I have the clipping in my scrapbook. I told the writer, "I'm a reformed eater. I weighed 245 pounds when I came to the Coast League. Now I'm down to 195. But I'll have to diet the rest of my life. If I don't I'll weigh 280."

I wasn't even close. I was about 75 pounds shy.

*   *   *

The players are very quick to pick up on weight gain. And since the day they first started to ride me about it, they've never let up. Some of it I take very well, some not so well, depending on the circumstances and the person.

I think the first "fat" nickname I got was "Rerun," after a character from the *What's Happening* TV show. Bill Madlock gave it to me. "Tons of Fun" was another one.

Pete Rose, then with the Phillies, said, "What time does the balloon go up?"

One day someone told me that my girlfriend would be arriving at the park in the fifth inning.

I'm thinking, "What girlfriend? I don't have a girlfriend."

Then in the fifth inning the Goodyear blimp flew overhead.

Things were getting rough. I couldn't keep away from the table. They called me Fat Albert. The Mets' players would yell "Hey, hey, hey" when I took the field.

As I say, if it's in good fun, I could go with it. But one time, when Madlock was with the Giants, his manager, Dave Bristol, yelled from the dugout, "Bear down, Rerun." There was nothing good-natured about that at all. He took the nickname because he heard Madlock use it, and got on me. Believe me, I could tell the difference between good-natured and a cheap shot from a bad guy.

I ran Bristol out of the game for that.

That might sound excessive (he thought so), but an umpire has a perfect right to heave somebody if he's making fun of you. It's a matter of respect for the uniform, respect for the representative of the league office, and establishing your authority on the field. Contrary to what you hear all the time, you don't have to swear or say the "magic words" to get ejected.

Bristol came charging out, as I knew he would.

"How come Madlock can say Rerun all the time and you don't do nuthin', and I say it and you toss me?" he asked.

This was the last game of the season, no less.

So I tell Bristol that when Madlock does it, I know where it's coming from, just as I knew there was nothing nice in it when it came from him.

He went crazy at this point. He tore off his uniform shirt and threw it, and I told him, "That's one hundred dollars."

That's the fine for throwing equipment.

So he takes off his shoes—both of them—and I let him know that it's now up to three hundred dollars.

So off came his two socks, and he's now up to five hundred dollars. Finally, he gets smart and leaves. What a mess.

I write up my report and send it to Chub Feeney, but Feeney reduces the fine in half, giving him some sort of credit for the shoes and socks only counting as one piece of equipment or something. I called Richie Phillips to complain about the reduced fine, but nothing ever came of that.

Dallas Green was the man who presented me with my Most Likely to Succeed award in umpire school, when he was the Phillies' assistant farm director. Now he was the Phils' manager, and we had our share of go-arounds.

He used to call me Fat Albert a lot, and he also had a couple of troublemakers on his team named Larry Bowa and Tug McGraw. Bowa was just a bad guy, while McGraw had a reputation for being terrific, but he could be malicious. He would always be calling me "Cheeseburger" or "Quarter Pounder."

Once McGraw called me "Quarter Pounder" from the dugout, and I warned him to knock it off and not call me that again.

He said, "Okay, Hoagie."

Boom, I threw him out.

Same thing with Dallas Green. I told him not to call me Rerun anymore, but the next day he was imitating the Mets and repeating, "Hey, hey, hey."

Boom, I threw him out.

But in the right place, I could take it. I can even laugh about it. One day during a rain delay in Cincinnati, with the Reds losing, Rose was yelling at me to get the field covered.

So Tommy Lasorda, over in the Dodgers' dugout (no lightweight himself at the time), hollers, "Just throw Gregg's jacket over the field."

And someone in the Reds' dugout answers, "You can't do that because Eric Gregg's suit is going condo after the game!"

Most umpires disliked Larry Bowa, which the fans didn't really appreciate until he became a manager and got a bad reputation for arguing so much. But he was like that as a player too.

I know it's not polite to say you hate someone, but I can honestly say I hate Bowa. He's just misery. He argues everything: you say strike, he says ball, you say fair, he says foul, you say cover the field, he says the weather's fine. You come to expect that he'll go against anything you say just to be ornery. I can tell you, it didn't help his career any. He had a long and good career, and to his credit, he did it without making friends with any umpires.

Fans always want to know what players are like; I was always straight with them when it came to Larry Bowa.

Near the end of his career, he was playing for the

Cubs, and I was umpiring at first. We were at Wrigley
Field. Here comes this odd play where he's the batter,
and he runs into me and knocks me down. I was well
over three hundred pounds at the time; Bowa weighed
about half that. But I was standing still, and he was at
full speed, and it just happened.

I was seeing stars, and completely missed the call
at first. I just heard voices saying, "Safe or out,
safe or out?"

So I had the presence of mind to say, "Who's
asking?"

The answer was Bowa.

So all I say is, "Bowa's out."

I know I got that right.

The amazing thing was, just as Bowa's reputation
was at its worst, during his managing days at San Diego,
he was actually starting to get a little better. Not that
we were feeling sorry for him, but we all agreed he was
improving a little. Still, we all had a little pool going
about when he was gonna get it.

There was a lot of irony to his firing. First, it was
obvious it was coming any day; the Padres were doing
terribly, and the papers were filled with the rumors. It
was no secret the end was near.

The interesting thing was, his boss was Chub Feeney, who after leaving as National League president,
where he'd been the umpires' boss, had become general manager at San Diego. And we all knew how tough
Chub could be. Very.

So now Chub is the man with the axe over
Bowa's head.

The way Bowa got fired was really bad, to tell you
the truth. He didn't even know. The writers told him
about it. Finally, Feeney called him to come up to
his room.

Bowa said, "Is this to tell me I'm fired?"

Chub said "yes."

So Bowa said, "Then we've got nothing to talk about."

And that was it for Bowa's managing career, at least as this is being written.

As for Feeney, he was the guy who once fined Garry Templeton a few grand for making an obscene gesture on the field. Now, he's running Templeton's team, the Padres. And the end came for Chub later that season when *he* made an obscene gesture to the fans, who were all over his case, from his seat at Jack Murphy Stadium. And then Feeney was fired.

What a game. It's like they say, whatever goes around comes around.

My weight was still soaring. My suit jacket was up to a 56 long and by 1980 my weight was at 354. My collar was a 22½. And I knew it was out of control.

The kidding continued, but I was getting a little more sensitive to it.

Joe Torre, when he was managing the Mets, came out to argue one day over a trapped ball by Dave Kingman.

"If you'd lose a little weight," he said, "you could cover the ground a little better."

"Joe," I answered, "I was on top of that play. I was right there."

"Listen, Eric," he said, before heading back to the dugout. "I'm going to send you a copy of that play on tape for Christmas."

Dick Williams told the press that "his strike zone is as big as his rear end."

I didn't appreciate that.

Dave Bristol said he wanted my old uniforms to use as horse blankets.

Greg Gross of the Phillies, at Shea Stadium one day, when I couldn't find a ball: "Eric, if it was two scoops you'd find it in a second."

Tony Perez and Mario Soto used to call me "Chuleta," which meant "pork chop."

In my first season, I'd have to say Frank Pulli and Bruce Froemming were the biggest help to me. I molded myself after Froemming. He took care of me; taught me how to deal with tough situations. He'd say, "You can always tone an umpire down, but you can never light a fire under him."

Pulli taught me a lot about positioning, getting the plays right, being in the right spot to make the call.

Froemming can be a character. One day he got on our plane a few minutes ahead of me. Calm as can be, he told the stewardess he'd prefer if no black people sat with him. Just like that.

Of course, she didn't know what to say, so she just hoped it didn't happen, and being first class, it's probably not going to.

Well of course, I didn't know that any of this has gone on, so I go aboard, all 350 pounds of me, and I sat myself in my assigned seat, right next to Bruce.

I was a little loud that day to begin with, and now Froemming starts motioning to the stewardess and making faces, like she's supposed to remove this 350-pound black guy from his seat because Froemming requested "no black people."

She doesn't know what to do, but at least she thinks she can tell me to keep the noise down. And she does.

That really pissed me off, and I'm starting to get mad at her when Froemming and Dick Stello start laughing and laughing and I realize the whole thing has been set up. I felt bad for the stewardess, but she was relieved that it was all a joke.

These things happened to me a lot. Another standard trick was that a partner would get into our hotel a moment before me and quickly whisper to the room clerk, "Don't put Eric Gregg on my floor."

I'd get there a second later, say, "I'm Eric Gregg," and the clerk would frantically be trying to change rooms. All the while, I'm wondering why everyone else had a key waiting and I'm standing there while they fumbled around behind the desk.

I'm a good-natured guy, but to be honest, there are times when life on the road can be lonely. I was the only black in the league, and so much younger than the other guys. I really had to make my own friends in each town, and often go off by myself. Fortunately, I had the kind of personality where I could do just that, but a lot of times there were just lonely nights in the room with the TV set.

It was especially true in my first few years, though, that I had to be careful not to flaunt my contacts, and rather, to know my place. It was like the Jerry Smith lesson from that spring training game: Don't be a hotshot in front of all these veterans.

Once we were in Cincinnati, where they just have the best late-night fried chicken room service. I've got HBO on the TV, room service ordered, and I'm all set for a great night. '

Room service knocked on the door, and I was already licking my chops. Come on in!

I opened the cover and there was nothing but chicken bones on the plate with a note from Froemming. It said, "Thought you were on a diet."

The next night, my partners went off to a fine rib restaurant in Cincy. Maybe the best ribs in the league. And I told Froemming, "Listen, I'm gonna be watching TV; bring me back a slab of ribs."

So off they go to dinner, and I'm passing the time, looking at the clock, figuring out how long it should take them to get served and get back to the hotel with my ribs. And each half hour seems like three, and those ribs are starting to get tastier and tastier.

Back come the guys, there's a knock on the door and a takeout bag on the floor. I open it up, pop open the cover, and wham, more bones.

I went to Froemming's room and threw the bones at him. But it was part of the initiation, I suppose.

There were two other special events in my rookie season that stood out.

Eric Joseito Gregg was born on August 17, 1978, our first child. We were now a family, I had more responsibilities than ever, and more to the point, I was determined to be a good father, even if my job required so much time away from home.

My own father had never paid much attention to my career. Frankly, I didn't think he gave a damn about it at all, probably thinking I was headed nowhere. But despite all the grief he caused my mother, I still loved him. And I knew the lessons of my own childhood, and anytime I might have an argument with Conchita now, I still say to myself, "Eric, hold on. Don't make this home like your childhood home." And it helps me sort things out.

I was working at Veterans Stadium one day in that summer of '78, right around the time little Eric was born. Chris Wheeler, the Phillies' announcer, got permission to place a cordless mike on me to use some sound for the Phillies highlight film.

So, I'm wired. And I'm working with Pulli, Doug Harvey, and Nick Colosi, and my aunt called to say she was bringing someone special to the game. The other umps knew about it.

We're at home plate doing the ground rules and lineups, when Pulli points into the stands and I see this guy waving at me. It was my father! I never expected him to ever come to see me work. I was so happy, I waved back like crazy, my eyes got twice their size, and it was all captured and used on the Phillies highlight film for 1978, which was a year they won the division title.

He's never been back since that day, but I was proud to have him there then, and I'll always remember it.

CHAPTER SEVEN

Strike!

YOU COULD SEE the strike of 1979 coming after that one-day strike in 1978.

Although I was still just a young rookie umpire then, by 1979 I was a Richie Phillips man all the way. Like Barney Deary a few years earlier, Richie became like a father figure to me. He was tough, he could overwhelm you in discussions, but he was obviously the right man for us in these times. Now, the painful reality was clear to us; a strike in 1979 seemed likely, and we'd better expect it.

By my second year, my salary was $17,500. The highest-paid umpires in baseball that year were Nester Chylak, Ed Vargo, Doug Harvey, and Bill Haller, each at $38,000. It was not a lot of money when you consider the responsibility that went with it and that there were only fifty-two major league umpiring jobs in America. Obviously, some extraordinary skills went with the job, certainly enough to command better pay. NBA officials with ten years' experience were making $45,000 for an eighty-two-game schedule. We were representing the American and National League offices, the only people at the ballpark, aside from the official scorer, paid by Major League Baseball.

No one was claiming that the umpires should be paid like the players, but their salaries were climbing tremendously since the Andy Messersmith/Dave McNally free agency decision in 1976. Baseball players were now approaching a million dollars a year. Surely there had to be a fairer way to compensate the umpires.

Although the courts had ruled that our union's agreement with baseball was valid, Richie Phillips's strategy in 1979 was to acknowledge that fact, but to have each of us retain him as individual counsel, negotiating our contracts one by one. The union agreement set minimum pay standards, but did not require that each ump receive the minimum. When the league presidents, Feeney and MacPhail, went back to the same courtroom that upheld them in '78, they were told that this time Phillips was right. We were permitted to bargain our own contracts individually.

This was a major breakthrough. It was also the start of a long and unpleasant stalemate. Spring training was now here, and none of us, except for Ted Hendry of the American League (who had signed a two-year contract the year before) and Paul Pryor of the National League, reported to work. The teams had to scramble to find replacement umpires for the exhibition games.

One of the saddest turns to this was that my old friend and mentor Barney Deary, who was on Major League Baseball's payroll to run the Umpire Development Program, was enlisted to help stock the games with substitutes. This cast Barney in the enemy camp. Obviously, he had to do what he had to do. But it was very painful for me to see my dear friend on the other side. It put a strain on our relationship, and on his relationship with many other umpires as well, a strain that never really healed. I regret that deeply to this day.

Except for Hendry (who Phillips acknowledged had to work), and Pryor, all fifty of us flew to Chicago on

March 30 to hear directly from Phillips where we stood.

Phillips reviewed the situation. We were holding firm on our strategy; none of us had signed contracts for 1979. The union was also demanding that additional umpires be added to the staffs to allow midseason vacations for the umpires. This didn't seem unreasonable. We were away from our families for seven solid months. The job should not take with it such an infringement on efforts to maintain a marriage. Believe me, the divorce rate was pretty high among the umpires. It was a tough life on their wives.

Pryor, an eighteen-year veteran, had signed a two-year contract a couple of weeks earlier. A lot of our talk was about him, and the hiring of the substitutes. That was another ugly side to the mess.

It was really the younger guys who were going to carry this to its conclusion. To tell you the truth, the veteran umpires went along, and knew it was to everyone's benefit, and they were the kinds of guys who wouldn't desert you when the going got tough. But I know their hearts weren't in it. They were men of great loyalty, and for so many years their loyalty had been to baseball and to the American and National Leagues. Now it was being painfully tested. Richie understood that, and helped the older umpires deal with that.

We were making no progress and it was obvious that the regular season was going to open without us. That hurt. We liked to think that they couldn't play without us, and we had no doubt that the quality of the game would be affected. The league offices had always proudly boasted that we were the crème de la crème, the people who made Major League Baseball the beautifully played, honest, superbly officiated sport that it was. Baseball was the nation's number one pastime for a lot of reasons, and the quality of the officiating was one of them.

I was fortunate to have my old job at the engraver's to go back to. But as the weather turned nice, and baseball fever was in the air, everyone I worked with knew how much I was hurting. I had worked so long and so hard to get where I was. Now, reading the statements by Chub Feeney and Lee MacPhail, I was wondering if it was all over.

We had gotten individual letters before spring training telling us that we would risk losing our jobs if we didn't report. And now as the regular season was approaching, the leagues announced that they would hire, and sign to contracts, minor league umpires who were not part of the union. These would be men who would be taking our jobs, and don't think it didn't occur to each of us that our jobs might be gone forever.

Richie assured us that this was not going to be the case; that we had to hold firm. The game could not take the blow to its integrity that replacement umpires would eventually bring. They might get by for a few days or a few weeks, and it was expected that players and managers would be pretty patient with them, but eventually, the seasoning they were lacking would start to show up in crucial situations. The integrity of the pennant race could be in danger over one bad game. We knew the league presidents would be holding their breaths against the inevitable.

Of the first dozen umpires at the Triple-A level who were offered big league contracts, we understood that nine said no. Another umpire, Bill Emslie, considered the best prospect in the minors, was never even asked. He was an active supporter of the union from his vantage point in the minors, and actively campaigned to stop minor league umpires from taking scab jobs. For the nine who said no, their opportunity might never come again. It would not be forgotten that they took that courageous action. It would not be forgotten by the

league officials, who waited years before giving them
their big league shot, nor by the striking umpires, who
forever viewed them as heroes. Emslie was fired after
the 1981 season when league officials said neither major league was interested in him. He was rehired in '82
and then fired again after the season. He was reinstated
in May of 1983 after a National Labor Relations Board
hearing was requested by the Umpires Association. But
his day in the sun never came. Emslie finally made it
to the big leagues in 1988, when George Steinbrenner
hired him as the team's traveling secretary. But between 1979 and 1987, we never had an umpire's meeting without someone saying, "What about Emslie?"

As for the "refuseniks," they eventually made it, but
it took more years than it should have. Drew Coble, Bob
Davidson, Gerry Davis, Dan Morrison, Rocky Roe, Randy
Marsh, Charlie Williams, and Mark Johnson were the
men. Roe came up in '81, Coble, Marsh, and Williams
(another black umpire) in '82, Davidson and Morrison
in '83, Johnson in '84, and Davis not until 1985.

Those Triple-A umpires who became replacement
umpires were John Shulock, Fred Spenn, Dallas Parks
(my old partner in the barber shop), Derryl Cousins,
Lanny Harris, Steve Fields, my old umpire school
classmate Dave Pallone, and Fred Brocklander. Barney
supplied two of his instructors, retired umps Mike
Fitzpatrick and Dick Nelson, and Dick Tremblay, another retired ump, rounded out the "crew chiefs." The
other umpires would be local amateurs.

I knew most of these men from the minors, spring
training, umpire development school, instructional
leagues, and winter ball. Some had been my friends.
Some were even close friends. That could never be the
same again. They were now the scabs who were breaking our strike lines, taking our jobs, making our stand

tougher. Each had his own reasons. The chance to be a major league umpire, the added pay, the sudden rise to the top when it was completely unexpected. They knew there would be a price tag on their actions, and I'm sure each man gave it a lot of thought. I can't guarantee you that every one of the fifty striking umpires would have said "no" if offered a similar opportunity under similar circumstances. Probably a number of us would have said yes. I'd like to think I would have said no, but unless you're faced with the decision, it's easy to think you'd go the right way. I just don't know. I had a wife and a child, and my dream was to work in Major League Baseball.

Anyway, my dream was getting very cloudy. I was spending my days doing the dastardly deed of printing up our strike signs. They were in the shape of chest protectors and said things like "Baseball Unfair to Umpires," and "Baseball Is Killing the Umpires" and some worse stuff directed at "MacFeeney and MacPhail." I'm glad they never found out who was actually printing up those signs.

We had hoped that the Players Association might back us and honor our picket line, but that was hoping for too much. The games were going to go on, without us.

After working two games, Paul Pryor had a change of heart and decided to join us. But Phillips told him to get back to work—by signing a two-year contract and then by walking, he'd be in a lot more trouble than we were. Still, his action helped his relationship with us.

On April 16, Hendry quit his American League job. He told MacPhail he couldn't stand working with the inferior quality umpires. The league added Bill Lawson to its staff to replace him. Paul Pryor, after ten days, was back out with us again.

This was killing a lot of guys. The umpire supervisors in both leagues were former umps, whose sympathies were undoubtedly with us, but whose loyalty had to be to the offices they now worked out of. Tom Gorman, Ed Sudol, Al Barlick, Ken Burkhart, Emmett Ashford, Nester Chylak (who had retired in 1978), Hank Soar, and John Stevens were all posted on duty at the games with the scab and amateur umpires. It was ugly and sad.

There were picket lines outside the ballparks and we were on all the newscasts. In Cleveland and San Diego, amateur umpire associations refused to staff games. That was classy. In San Diego, they managed to come up with only four replacement umpires, while most cities worked from a pool of eight or ten. In Pittsburgh, a strong union town, union officials urged fans to stay away during strike games. The Pirates then drew under eleven thousand for helmet day and three thousand and twelve for Easter Sunday. We were beginning to feel like we might win.

Phillips met with Feeney and MacPhail on April 21 in Princeton, New Jersey. The leagues agreed not to cut off our medical benefits, which would have expired the following week. Richie thought progress was being made.

The same day, there was the chaos on the field we were hoping would come. The patience of the managers had worn out. In a real mess of a game, Joe Torre of the Mets and Joe Altobelli of the Giants both filed protests after umpires reversed themselves twice and caused a twenty-eight-minute argument. On May 9, four managers, five players, and a coach were ejected in various games as patience continued to dwindle among the pros.

By now, the club owners were seeing diminished quality in their games. Newspaper columnists were saying that fans were paying full price for tickets and not seeing true Major League Baseball. On May 17, following a fourteen-hour negotiating session in New York, an agreement was reached. The next day, we all met in Philadelphia, heard Richie recommend to take it, and voted our approval. The forty-five-day strike was over.

What did we get?

We got our vacations: one week in the first year, and two weeks after that, including travel pay home and back.

Our pension plan was extended from 1979 to 1982.

Our spring training pay went from $40 a game to $50 a game with the per diem raised to $55.

Our per diem during the regular season went from $51 to $67 in 1979, and up to $72 in 1980 and $77 in 1981 instead of the $1 a year increase.

Salaries would now start at $22,000 in the first year and go to $28,000 in the fifth, $38,000 in the tenth, and $45,000 in the 15th.

In the event of a players' strike, we would receive up to forty-five days of full pay. (This would be a big one.)

National League crew chiefs got an extra thousand dollars, the same as American League crew chiefs were already getting.

We gave in on postseason selections, allowing the leagues to select umpires for the playoffs and World Series based on merit, not on a rotation, but assuring that no one would get more than one such assignment in any given year, no one would get it two years in a row, or twice in three years.

There were other benefits included for us, and they agreed that "there would be no retribution against any of the umpires who walked the picket line."

I definitely came out ahead over time, if not in that first year, and the union was a big winner by sticking together, gaining renewed respect from everyone who had never appreciated their talents before, and establishing itself as a legitimate part of the baseball family.

Richie Phillips did well for us, and well for himself, as he earned a percentage of each umpire's salary. There was some grumbling about that, but most felt he had earned it.

Meanwhile, to accommodate the new vacation schedules, and to fulfill promises made to the replacement umpires, the American League permanently added Shulock, Spenn, Parks, and Cousins to its staff, and the National League added Harris, Fields, Pallone, and Brocklander.

These men would become known as the Scab Umpires. This would be a problem for baseball that would not go away.

Here we were, back to work after a very bitter strike, suddenly assigned to work with the people who had jeopardized our position and our careers, and who in fact had agreed to take our jobs. In the tiny confines of umpire locker rooms beneath the big major league stadiums, we were told to welcome these people as new umpires and work with them.

This was not an easy assignment. By nature, umpires are an all-for-one-and-one-for-all group of strong-willed bodies. To ask us to embrace the scabs was unrealistic. The league offices had to know that, but they felt obligated to the minor league guys who had bailed them out and allowed the games to go on. And they had given them major league contracts to do it.

At one of our meetings, when we ratified the agreement, we discussed the scabs. There was a lot of anger in the room. And we basically said, "This is how it's gonna be." We wouldn't let them hang. We'd help them on the field. But off the field, they had to handle whatever came up themselves. If they couldn't handle it, they shouldn't be umpires in the first place. An ump has to be able to handle human relationships, for good or for bad. We had to remember that some deserving guys lost jobs because of these people, guys who were ready for the majors but were now at the back of the line, with inferior guys having moved ahead of them because they were scabs.

I suppose the league officials could have hired all amateurs, who would have gone away after the settlement and never been heard from again. Now, they were burdened by the presence of these guys who were not qualified to work in the majors, but who were there, perhaps for decades, like it or not.

I had no love for the scabs, but I had to wonder how it would have been for me. Imagine being a scab and the only black umpire. Talk about feeling outside. I used to laugh and tell Dick Stello, "Half you guys don't like me now; can you imagine if I was also a scab?"

Some nasty things were done to the scabs, to be sure. First of all, no one would associate with these guys off the playing field. If they needed assistance on the field, we never let them hang out to dry. That would have compromised our own professionalism, because working as a team to get the calls right is the way things are done. But once we left the playing field, these people might as well have not existed. We didn't associate with them in the locker rooms, the hotels, the airports, or the restaurants. We wouldn't give them the time of day. Some guys made their lives extra tough by canceling their plane reservations before they got to the airports, and found other fiendish ways to screw things up for them. Signs were tacked to their lockers and their luggage that said "SCAB." It got ugly, and I'd be lying if I didn't say I could feel for them from time to time.

They had families, they had the same desire to reach the majors as I had, and they were now in this awful position. I guess most of them understood that it went with their decision, but I could never bring myself to respect that decision or them.

Over the years, tensions eased a little. But the strike and the scabs will never go away from memory. Pallone and Parks, two of my minor league buddies, were now scab umpires before they were anything else. And even if I didn't quite fit in with my colleagues on other matters, I was bound to stay with them on this one.

Ringing up Gary Carter at Shea Stadium in New York in 1989. Mike LaValliere is the Pittsburgh catcher. *Photograph by Keith Torrie, New York* Daily News

My boyhood home on Pallas Street in West Philadelphia. My father still lives there. *Author's personal collection*

Above left, the sandlot across the street from my home, where we'd play ball after school. *Right,* this photo is from high-school graduation in 1968. I was the first member in my family to graduate. You wouldn't know it from the celebration, but I was very shy. *Below,* at a banquet with former Miss America Suzette Charles   *Author's personal collection*

Vice-president George Bush visited the umpires before the 1986 All-Star Game in Houston. Left to right are Steve Palermo, Bruce Froemming, Tim McClelland, Mr. Bush, Paul Runge, Rick Reed, myself, and our attorney, Richie Phillips. *Photograph courtesy of The White House*

Right, the honor of working the first night game in the history of Wrigley Field went to (left to right) Jim Quick, myself, Larry Poncino, and Dave Pallone. *Author's personal collection*

Top left, on the set of my favorite soap opera, *The Young and the Restless,* I got to meet Ilene Davidson, who plays Ashley Abbott. My wife and I named our daughter after Ilene's character. *Author's personal collection*

Right, Barney Deary, the man who took me under his wing and guided me into the umpiring profession *Photograph by Lou Dreary*

Left, the famous hamburger on third base in St. Louis in 1988. I almost took a bite, then decided against it. *Photograph by Ted Reisinger*

It didn't matter that it was my own son. A strike is a strike, and he was outta there.   *Author's personal collection*

Above, Conchita Gregg, the best thing that ever happened to me.   *Author's personal collection*

Left, when Pete Rose signed with the Phillies, I was among those who welcomed him to Philadelphia in 1979, following my first full season in the National League.   *Author's personal collection*

Top left, with Giants' quarterback Phil Simms on the banquet circuit *Author's personal collection*

Right, with Olympic star Carl Lewis, on the banquet circuit   *Author's personal collection*

Left, in the heat of the 1986 pennant race, Cincinnati's Eric Davis and the Mets' Ray Knight went at it, and I wound up holding Davis while Knight pummeled him.   *Author's personal collection*

This couldn't have been much of an argument with Mets' coach Bill Robinson.   *Author's personal collection. Below,* the umpiring crew and managers at the opening of the 1987 National League Championship Series: (left to right) Giants' manager Roger Craig, myself, Jim Quick, John Kibler, Ed Montague, Dave Pallone, Whitey Herzog of the Cardinals, and Bob Engle.   *Photograph courtesy of Herren Photography*

Clockwise from top, surrounding Conchita are Eric Joseito, Kevin Van Arsdale, Jamie Erin, and Ashley Gabrielle. My family. *Author's personal collection*

Below left, Conchita on the field at Candlestick Park immediately after the earthquake at the 1989 World Series *Author's personal collection*

Right, I was really proud to be selected as the 1989 Graduate of the Year from the Philadelphia Public Schools. Understandably, it was a terrific feeling of accomplishment. *Photograph by Hawk-Eye*

CHAPTER EIGHT
Here's the Beef

BY 1980, I was down to one situp a day.

Half when I woke up, and half when I went to bed.

I was getting tired of getting a shoeshine and taking the guy's word for it.

The New York Mets stuffed their jackets with towels and walked around yelling "out" and "safe" and there was no doubting who they were imitating.

The St. Louis Cardinals had a five-pound sandwich of cold cuts sent to my locker room before a game.

And the taunts of "Rerun," "Fat Albert," and "Tons of Fun" continued.

So did my diet of Philadelphia cheese steaks, burgers, mustard pretzels, beer, and ribs. I would have hamburgers and fried chicken as an appetizer before dinner.

First Conchita would get on me about it. I was becoming twice the man she married.

Then letters started arriving from Blake Cullen, the supervisor of umpires in the National League office, and from Chub Feeney. They weren't out-and-out warnings, but the message was clear: Shape up. It was bad for your health, and it was bad for the league's appearance.

But I didn't do anything about it. I knew I was hustling, I knew I was in position to make my calls, and I knew my ability wasn't affected one bit. So I didn't pay any attention to it.

Then little Kevin Van Arsdale Gregg was born on April 28, 1980. I had a cousin, Skip Wright, who was a ballboy for the Philadelphia 76ers basketball team, and when the twins, Tom and Dick Van Arsdale, played there, they were always nice to me. I think they took a liking to me. They'd slip me some extra soda, or let me dribble around a little. At umpire school I called myself Eric Van Arsdale Gregg during pickup basketball games. And I told my wife that I'd name a kid after them. Told them too. And I did.

Anyway, now I've got two children, and one day Harry Wendelstedt and Frank Pulli are talking to me about my weight. I don't know if the league office put them up to it or anything, but Harry said something that finally registered. He said I wouldn't be around to raise my two sons unless I lost some weight.

That lingered with me all season. One day Dallas Green poked me in the chest during an argument and a button popped on my jacket. It was embarrassing.

So when the season ended, I called Gus Hoefling, the Phillies' strength and flexibility coach, and asked him for help. I had tried health spas on and off, but they didn't help much. There was too much socializing there. I told him I needed to lose "a couple of pounds," but he knew the score. Ruly Carpenter, who owned the Phillies, gave me permission to use Veterans Stadium. I made arrangements to work under Gus's guidance, and to be sure to work out early so I wouldn't be fraternizing with any players who'd come around later on.

I weighed about 361.

Gus showed me a blank piece of paper and said

that that represented my new diet. So I ate the paper. He told me I had enough weight so that I could hibernate through the winter and survive with no problems.

But actually, he limited my red meat to about six ounces, three or four times a week. I was reduced to coffee and fruit juice at breakfast time, milk with added protein at lunch and vegetables for dinner. Gus told me to avoid salads because I'd pour dressing on them and that was high in calories. So I'd eat cucumbers and melons and bananas. I'd drink diet cola, but no beer. I'd have club soda or grapefruit juice, and sometimes even skip breakfast altogether. Let me tell you, it wasn't easy.

I'd watch all of my favorite soap operas and not be allowed to munch on anything while I sat there. And, he had me on a workout plan at the Vet that had me arriving at 10:15 each weekday morning, and going under his supervision until noon.

I'd do situps, pushups, weightlifting, walking and jogging the sets of the Vet; Gus taught me yoga and kung fu exercises for the days I wasn't with him, similar to the things Steve Carlton did. At the Stadium, I used the Nautilus equipment to lift weights, and I'd do situps and scissor kicks.

I made arrangements to use the gym facilities at the University of Pennsylvania. I used their pool. I pushed myself harder than I thought I ever could.

And I started to lose weight. I started to lose ten pounds a week.

My problem had always been that I was a nervous eater, a nosher. It wasn't that I would sit down and eat eleven pork chops. It wasn't so much the quantity as the eating habits I had developed. I was a closet eater, someone who'd order a pizza from room service in a hotel at three A.M.

I would have six or seven beers after a ball game. I

wouldn't walk enough. If I was umpiring at third base, I wouldn't get any exercise at all unless a play came to me. I was doing junk food and not exercising, and not giving any thought to proper eating habits. Gus was getting a handle on all of this for me.

At the end of fourteen weeks like this, I was down an incredible 106 pounds, to 255. By the time I went to spring training in 1981, I was the subject of all sorts of magazine stories, posing in my old size-56 jacket with room for two in there. I was now a 46. *Sports Illustrated* featured me. I was on the cover of *Ebony*. All the wire services reported on the new-look Eric Gregg.

Even players were shocked.

Jerry Royster wanted to know where the rest of me went. Gaylord Perry said, "Eric, you're looking good!" I didn't even know that he knew my first name.

I have to admit, I felt pretty good about myself. The bulk was probably tiring me out. I know I used to sweat a lot, and those rushes to catch airplanes weren't doing me any good.

The initial weight had made me a celebrity among umpires, but the weight loss made me pretty famous across the country. My before-and-after pictures were running all over the place.

I had gotten invited to a few banquets over the years; now the invitations were really pouring in. At the big winter baseball banquet in Pittsburgh, the "Dapper Dan Dinner," it was reported that "Eric literally stole the show." It led to a booking at the big winter dinner in Manchester, New Hampshire, and later Ken Kaiser's big bash in Rochester, New York. I'd tell the Mary Sue Styles story, some Larry Bowa stories, some Lasorda stories, and I'd be on a roll. I even hired Bowa's agent to book these dinners for me. I addressed an IBM executive gathering and was a guest on a number of TV shows. There was a long interview with me on the *CBS Morning News.*

In Philadelphia, where people recognized me on the street all the time, I started getting TV commercials. I did several commercials for Phillies Franks, one for a bank, and I did some promotional work for Continental Airlines. I even got my kids in the Phillies Franks commercials. They made one where I just said, "Hey, I lost 106 pounds and I still eat Phillies Franks." A feature story on me on the *Evening Magazine* television show on Channel 3 in Philadelphia eventually led to my own segments as a contributing reporter on that show. I did sports features, such as where they get the mud to rub up the baseballs, and things with the Eagles, 76ers, and Flyers.

In the cover story interview with *Ebony,* I said, "People have been extremely good to me, and I'm thankful for that. So many people have complimented me for taking off the weight that I'd feel like a fool if I put it on again. I want to get down to about 220 pounds and stay there."

It was easier said than done.

Life back on the road did not give me the opportunity to continue working with Gus Hoefling. And there were all those cheesburgers waiting for me in all those National League towns.

So try though I did, the weight began to come back. Not in one burst, but cheeseburger by cheeseburger, until the letters from the league office started to come in again. And by 1984 I was back over three hundred, and I am still fighting to get back under that. It's obvious that it will never be easy for me, but I've got to keep trying.

I was in a hotel with my family in New York in

1988 when I got chest pains. An ambulance came and I was taken to a hospital. It wasn't a heart attack, and I didn't miss many games, but I think somebody was trying to tell me something.

After that season, I was back on a vigorous conditioning and weight loss program. Bart Giamatti, the league president at the time, was very supportive. "The main thing is your good health," he told me, although he was smoking a cigarette when he did it. But he offered to pay for my weight rehabilitation, even to find me a weight reduction class in each National League city. But he was also the first one to ever flat out say, "If you don't trim down, we might have to let you go."

I've got to get a handle on this. I know this is serious.

Giamatti was really a fine man. With his educational background, it would have been easy for him to "talk down" to people, but he had a gift for communicating and was always very down to earth with us. He was the first league president I worked for who treated me like an equal. He'd take time for one-on-one talks. He'd ask our opinions on rules, on discipline, even on which umpires we would like to be teamed with.

He was very impressed when he learned that my children were going to Episcopal Academy in Philadelphia.

He would come back to visit us when he became commissioner in 1989. He was no longer our boss, and the easy exchanges were even easier. He really had that touch.

He came into our locker room smoking his cigarette, and we said to him, "Hey, you know the rules— no smoking in here."

And he'd laugh and say, "That's a National League rule—I'm the commissioner now, not the league president!"

He wore a sport shirt and sneakers when he visited us at Shea Stadium. He had two of his children with him and it was such a nice visit. He talked about Lee Weyer, who had died the previous year, and he looked at me and told me to watch my weight, but always, the cigarette was there.

The Friday before Labor Day in 1989, I was in San Diego, sitting at the bar of a Mexican restaurant. A guy was complaining because I had asked the bartender to switch to the afternoon soaps.

Suddenly a news bulletin came on the TV screen. "From Cape Cod, Massachusettes, this just in . . . Baseball Commissioner A. Bartlett Giamatti, who just nine days ago banished Pete Rose from baseball over a betting scandal, has suffered a heart attack at his vacation home. The commissioner was taken unconscious to a nearby hospital. We will have further details as they become available."

He was already dead as they were reading the bulletin. He never regained consciousness and within a few hours, the news reported his death at age fifty-one. They mentioned that he was a heavy smoker.

I'm old enough now to have experienced a number of deaths close to me. That one was among the most unexpected, and among the saddest. It was a terrific loss for baseball, which could only have benefited by having such a man of high caliber in that office. Along with Richie Phillips and a number of other umpires, I attended a very moving memorial service at New York's Carnegie Hall for Mr. Giamatti two months after his death, a final farewell to a great man.

CHAPTER NINE

On the Home Front

ALTHOUGH I WAS by now a well-traveled, fairly independent guy, problems at home were always on my mind. There were times I felt three thousand miles away—which I often was, but there were times home seemed all very real, all very much a part of me. I always thought of myself as a family man, even if my childhood exposure to that kind of life wasn't very positive.

Although my parents had long ago split, it was probably for the best. No longer did my father have to vent his drunken anger at Mom or the kids. They lived apart, but close enough together so that in a strange way, I still thought of it as a family unit.

Mom got sick in the mid-1980s. She developed serious kidney problems. And I was pleased to discover that my dad was there for her, getting closer to her at her time of need. Age can do that. I'm sure he regretted a lot about what had gone down in the past. It became a time for making amends, and he was a man about it. He was up to the task.

My sister Karen still lives in The Bottom, in a very very dangerous and tough section. It hasn't been easy for her, but she's been a survivor. She helps care for

Mom, and she's become a grandmother herself, although she never got married. And her son Derek, my nephew, has turned into quite a basketball player, averaging 21 points a game for his college team. He's on scholarship.

My sister Cheryl lived in this awful apartment building in The Bottom where they now have armed guards at the door. All you have to do is drive by it to see what little chance you have in life when you call this place home.

I knew Cheryl was into drugs, but I didn't know how badly. When my parents split up, she was the support of the family. She always managed to have a pretty decent job. Her boyfriend, a fellow named Jackson, had some money and was nice to our family. They lived together, upstairs from my mother. I'm not even sure she knew how heavily Cheryl was getting involved in cocaine.

I came back home one fall after the season and couldn't believe what I saw. It was hardly Cheryl. She was completely out of it. One day she'd have this far-off look, another day she'd be going through withdrawal. I noticed this in 1985 and 1986. Mom was helpless to get control of this of course, and she just tried to assure me that Cheryl was okay, and was taking care of herself. I began to realize it was a lot worse than she was admitting.

Then Cheryl got into this pipe thing, smoking bad stuff through pipes, and just going further and further downhill.

I was in Los Angeles, summer of '87. I got a message to call Conchita.

"Eric," she said, "it's Cheryl, and it's bad. She's in a coma. You better come home."

She and a girlfriend were doing heroin. They were

found in an old car near that bad apartment building. People tried to tell me it was a car crash, but the truth was too apparent. There were a lot of different stories; maybe we'll never know what really happened, but when you look back at the poor girl's history, you'd have to know that if it didn't happen from drugs on that day, it would have happened eventually.

She was in a coma for four days. Her eyes were in the back of her head, but she looked beautiful to me as she lay there in the hospital. I filled with tears each time I visited her. Conchita held my hand and then let me cry onto her shoulder. Maybe if I hadn't been on the road so much . . . but hey, I was the kid brother. What in the world could I really have done?

She was only thirty-seven when she died.

Everyone knew Cheryl. You never saw a funeral so packed. So many friends from childhood were there. Richie Phillips was good enough to come. It was one of the biggest funerals I ever went to. Standing room only. The whole weekend of the funeral, everyone talked about how wonderful Cheryl was and how much she'd be missed.

I stayed for a week. The league was great to me. They'd never had an umpire come up from the ghetto before, and all of this had to be new on them, but they told me to do whatever I had to do, and come back when I was ready.

I supported Mom and Dad as best I could and then went back to work, thousands of miles away from The Bottom.

Maybe Cheryl never had a chance at all.

Since I went away in 1971, I'd never been able to get close to my brother Ernie. This made me sad, because I would have really enjoyed a close friendship with him. I admired him. He was a better baseball player than I was, and maybe he could have used baseball as a ticket out.

But when he was young, he got a taste of fast money. He started hanging out with bad people, and found the cash quick and easy. He was walking around with thousands of dollars in his pocket. Suddenly, he's wearing fine clothes, buying Mom a new car, a mink coat.

Mom was no fool. She knew he was up to no good. But again, without a father in the house, she could only control the situation so much. And Ernie was pretty much leading his own life, not even coming home every night. There was only so much you could do.

There were drugs to be bought and sold, guns to be used for protection, robberies to commit. It was his chosen way of life. And it caught up with him, as it had to eventually, and he was sent off to prison.

If you can believe this, Ernie then fell in with the wrong crowd in prison. I didn't think there were good crowds and bad crowds in the slammer, but he found the bad one. And even in prison, where we thought at least he was safe, he got into a drug dealing ring.

Soon he was in debt to the wrong guys. And one night, while he was sleeping, his cell was firebombed. He was burned over 90 percent of his body. We thought we had lost him for sure.

I went to visit him in the hospital. He was wrapped up like a mummy. There was no recognizing him. Even when the bandages came off, he was so badly scarred for life that it was a pathetic situation. Again, I had to cry at what I saw. Again, Conchita was my support through this crisis.

In the hospital, Ernie told me how he realized he'd screwed up his entire life.

"I'm messed up forever" was how he put it.

Plastic surgery would improve his condition a little, but not very much. He was freed from prison after the accident, left out in the streets to try and pick up his miserable life. Again, he never had a chance.

It wasn't long after that he got picked up for gun possession, a parole violation. And he's back in jail again for a twenty-year stretch.

In a way, we thought he might be better off. At least we knew he was alive, fed, and with a roof over his head. We didn't think about prison riots, which would come later, while I was umpiring in the World Series. It's a bad way to rationalize his situation, but you have to play the hand you're dealt. Ernie and I come from the same parents, the same upbringing. Baseball saved me. The fast money on the streets destroyed him.

Maybe he never had a chance either.

But Conchita and I were making a life for ourselves and our children. Ashley Gabrielle Gregg, my first daughter, was born on September 24, 1985. Jamie Erin Gregg was born at five P.M. on New Year's Eve in 1986, right to the minute of our twelfth wedding anniversary.

Conchita: I call her "warden" sometimes, because she's on my case all the time about staying in line, and God love her, she's just what I need. She's a great wife, a great mother, and an inspiration to everyone who meets her. Considering how fast we got married, I think I made an awfully good choice with her. And I think she did pretty good too.

We bought a home in the pretty Wynnefield Heights section of Philadelphia in 1981, the year of the players' strike. The timing was tough, since we didn't get paid for the full length of the strike, and when you get a new house, you need a lot of steady money flowing in. Also, I was hoping to work the League Championship Series that fall, and that was several thousand dollars I was counting on toward the house. As it was, all the work I did during the strike was a benefit softball game for St. Vincent's Child Abuse Center in Atlantic City with some Phillies and some Eagles players participating.

Anyway, the house is a corner house with a big backyard where the kids can play ball. Conchita says they tear up the lawn, but hey. . . .

Wynnefield Heights is predominantly a white area, certainly not very black. When we moved in, we started to get postcards and letters, written in a childlike scribble, warning us to get out of the neighborhood. I looked at them and said to Conchita, "Can you believe this?"

So we contacted the police and the FBI, and they told us, "Look, if someone's gonna blow you up, they don't send a postcard first." But that wasn't reassuring enough, especially with two kids in the house, and me on the road, and for a while we had cops stationed outside the house as a precaution.

But that nonsense passed long ago. We're happily settled in now, with fine neighbors and a great life-style. We had enough room so that in 1989, we were able to bring Conchita's brother up from the Dominican Republic with his little nine-month-old daughter, who needed surgery to correct a heart defect. We had the surgery done at the Hospital of the University of Pennsylvania, where they did an outstanding job. That little baby is doing fine now, and I'm so glad we could open our doors to them and get them the attention they needed.

As I get more seniority, I can take vacation time in midsummer, and I've actually been able to spend a July 4th weekend with my family. Let me tell you, we're not many miles from The Bottom, but it all seems a long way off when you're outside barbecuing some chicken on a sunny Sunday afternoon.

Not long ago, Conchita and I decided to convert

the family from Catholic to Episcopalian. The kids were in the choir at the Episcopal Church, and we hadn't been married as Catholics, so we went ahead and did it.

I guess one of the best-known things about me is my association with the Phillie Phanatic, their huge green mascot. Kids certainly know me for this, and that's what's beautiful about the mascot and the association; it's got kids at a very young age becoming aware of baseball.

The Phanatic was "born" in 1978, the creation of Bill Giles of the Phillies, and an answer to the famous San Diego Chicken. Every team tried to come up with an answer to the Chicken, but the Phillies did the best job.

During that '78 season, I was working at the Vet and the game was on the NBC *Game of the Week* telecast across the country. Between innings, the character motioned for me to dance with him.

This being my rookie season, there was no way I was going to do that, but Doug Harvey, our crew chief, nodded that it was okay. Well, the rock music was on, the Phanatic had rhythm, so what the heck. It wasn't planned, it just happened. And everyone had a great time, lots of laughs, and good wholesome publicity.

Dave Raymond works inside the character, and he's terrific. I can always tell when it's him or a substitute. We became such a good dance act that we made the January page of the 1989 Phillies calendar.

Now I'm a pinup calendar boy right on the refrigerator in my own house. My kids think it's terrific.

The only thing is, the league is always trying to cut back on this sort of thing. When it gets out of hand— when the mascots abuse the umpires and make fools of them—that's no good. We got a report once that one of the mascots urinated on an umpire! Sometimes they spill water on them or kick them in the rear or pull their hats off. I know what the league means. You have to retain your dignity. And if they address the problem to the individual teams, I think this can be controlled and we can still have a good time and help entertain the crowd.

In 1988, I was in St. Louis to work a Cardinals-Mets series. They always serve outstanding cheeseburgers in the locker room at Busch Stadium, often served up by the Cardinals trainer, Gene Gieselmann. On this particular day, I noticed that Gieselmann left our locker room one cheeseburger short, and I could swear I saw it sticking out of his pocket as he left the room.

The game is about to start, and I move out to the third base line. I'm getting ready for the national anthem when all the fans near me started to wave. So hey, I wave back. I'm a friendly guy. Now I notice that all the Mets players in the third base dugout are laughing, especially Roger McDowell, who's pointing to third base. And my umpire partner, Jim Quick, is pointing there too.

Well, what do you know. There, sitting right smack in the middle of that third base is one of the tastiest-looking cheeseburgers I had ever seen. Everyone was laughing, so I was a good sport too. I walked over, picked it up, started to take a bite, and then thought better of it.

Tom Lawless of the Cardinals had snuck it out there in his glove, and I couldn't be sure it was in mint condition, so I decided to let the joke end right there. I probably lost out on a good cheeseburger in the process.

CHAPTER TEN

A Tough Day at the Office

MY MOST FAMOUS GAME, even more famous than the Mary Sue Styles game, was a day (actually two days) working home plate in Wrigley Field, Chicago, August 17 and 18, 1982.

Someone sent me a headline from the Santa Monica *Evening Outlook* the next day. It read:

DODGERS WIN IN THE 21ST
Sax, Reuss and Gregg make it 2–1

It was not a pretty sight.

It all began innocently enough on a beautiful afternoon in Wrigley Field, Burt Hooton against Dickie Noles, twenty-seven thousand people on hand, Lee Elia managing the Cubs, and Lasorda, of course, the Dodgers.

The Cubs got a run in the first and the Dodgers tied it up in the second. Wrigley Field, you know, you sometimes figure you're in for a high-scoring game.

But on we went, 1–1, a good pitching duel, until the eighth inning. With one out, Larry Bowa singled for Chicago off Tom Niedenfuer. Then Leon "The Bull" Durham belted a double off the ivy wall in right field.

Pedro Guerrero fielded it, fired to the cutoff man Steve Sax, who threw a one-hopper to Mike Scioscia at home.

Scioscia had his left leg fully extended, blocking the plate. It's a tough act for anyone to score in that situation, especially a lightweight like Bowa. It's not easy to dislodge the leg.

The funny thing was, I had a play exactly like this one just five days earlier, my last game behind the plate. Joe Morgan was the runner, Scioscia the catcher, and Morgan was out.

Well, this was the same result. Bowa never got his foot in there, it was a bang-bang play, but I was on top of it. Bowa was out. The game remained tied at 1–1.

Bowa and Elia argued like hell. Of course, from the dugout, Elia had no way of seeing the play at all. I wound up throwing him out. It's a one-inch play in a cloud of dust: a question of whether someone gets his toe through Scioscia's leg and onto the plate or not. If Lee Elia can umpire a play like that from the dugout, he's in the wrong business. He should have been in umpire school with me.

Elia told the press, "No way Bowa was out."

Bad call, Lee. No way that you had a good view of it.

Bowa, of course, always argued about everything, and this was a potential game winner, so you can picture him in action. He wasn't a happy camper. Well, little did I know that destiny had it that we'd go into overtime, and on to seventeen innings before darkness forced us to suspend the game until the next day, still tied 1–1. So of course, all the morning papers focused on the play at the plate, all filled with Bowa's quotes. And I didn't hesitate to talk to the writers either. I told them that Scioscia's one of the best in the league at blocking the plate, and he did it perfectly on that play.

I don't think Scoscia helped the situation much, because he wasn't sure about it. He said, "I don't think Bowa got in, but I'm really not sure. I would have argued some if he was called safe. I don't think he got in because I think I had the plate blocked."

Well, now we're back at the ballpark the next day to resume play in the eighteenth inning. I'm dead tired, and we have a regularly scheduled game to follow the completion of the suspended game. I was just hoping this would end quickly and cleanly. And of course, I'm still behind the plate, because we're continuing where we left off.

But we went on for four more innings, twenty-one in all. Both teams pretty much cleaned out their rosters. The Dodgers even had Fernando Valenzuela playing the outfield, moving him between left and right depending on who was hitting.

Jerry Reuss, who was scheduled to pitch the regular game, had to come in to pitch in the 18th. (He wound up winning both ends of the "doubleheader.")

I wasn't the only one having a tough time. In the twentieth, Ron Cey was picked off first, and Dave Pallone had to eject both Cey and Lasorda for arguing. We were up to five ejections in the game, including both managers.

Now with one out in the top of the twenty-first, Sax doubled to right center and went to third on a wild pitch. Dusty Baker flied out to right, and Sax tagged up at third and headed for home.

Keith Moreland threw straight home where Jody Davis awaited the play. There was another cloud of dust, another bang-bang call to make. My right arm started to go up, my elbow was bent, and I was, frankly, overaggressive. But then my baseball instincts took over, the instincts that tell you after those thousands of games

whether the play is safe or out. Quickly, my arms flat-
tened and I yelled, "SAFE!"

Mayhem.

Billy Connors, acting Cub manager, was on top of
me before I even got up from my knees. The yelling
and the screaming, especially from the fans, was deaf-
ening. It was not my finest hour. I had the play correct,
but I wish I hadn't started to raise my right arm. Still,
the important thing was to get the call right, and I did.
No question.

Reuss retired the Cubs in the last of the twenty-first
and the game was in the record books. It was the longest game in innings in Wrigley Field history, the longest Cub game in time (six hours, ten minutes), and the
longest Los Angeles Dodgers game in innings. (The
Brooklyn Dodgers held the all-time record with a twenty-
six-inning game.)

Forty-five players appeared in the game, everyone
was whipped, and we still had another game to go. Fortunately, I would be at third base for that one.

But for Eric Gregg, the shouting wasn't over. The
Cubs held me to blame for Bowa being out in the eighth
and Sax being safe in the twenty-first. Somehow, it was
all my fault. Elia got the fans so mad that I thought I
was in physical danger, almost a Dominican Republic
situation. When the twenty-one-inning game ended I ran
off the field, because some fans had scaled the wall and
it looked like they were after me. Elia had incited them
with his attack in the newspapers, and then I had the
good fortune to have another play at the plate against
the Cubs to decide it.

It didn't end there. Harry Caray tore me up and
down on the Cubs broadcasts, and ESPN flat out said I
blew the call. For years, every time I was assigned to
Chicago, I could count on people writing threats on my

suitcases if they saw them sitting at the airport, the hotel, or even the ballpark.

A Dodger fan even mailed me a dollar bill and
thanked me for cheating against the Cubs!

Now *that* was a tough day at the office.

Seven years later, I was back at Wrigley Field, back
behind the plate, when another play loaded with con-
troversy came my way.

The date was September 23, 1989, and it was only
eight days after I'd been notified that I would be umpiring in my first World Series, so I was still on a high.
In addition, this particular game was being carried na-
tionally as one of the last NBC *Games of the Week*. I
had a lot of friends watching.

The Cubs were playing the Pirates and they hadn't
yet clinched the National League East, so this was an
important game for them.

In the last of the sixth, Mark Grace was up for the
Cubs with Dwight Smith on first. He took the first pitch
for a ball.

On the second pitch, Smith took off for second. The
pitch was in the dirt, and retrieved by the Pirates'
catcher, Dann Bilardello. Bilardello stood to chase the
ball and blocked my vision; Smith made it safely to second and I called the pitch a ball.

What I couldn't see was that Grace had, for some
reason, swung at the pitch. But nobody said a word. I
called for the baseball to make sure it was okay and
threw it back to the pitcher. Out loud, I said "two and
oh," and both Grace and Bilardello heard me. Grace
didn't say a word, knowing he'd gotten away with a
swing, and Bilardello was silent too. He hadn't seen the
swing either, for he was busy trying to block the
wild pitch.

Not a word was spoken by the Pirates' bench.

The scoreboard said one-and-one. The next pitch was a strike and I said, "two and one."

Now, Jim Leyland, the Pirates' manager, came running out and yelling, "No, no, it's not two and one, it's one and two! He swung at the wild pitch!"

My call at two and oh was quite clear. I said it out loud and I signaled with my hands.

I called time and went to speak with my partners. Jim Quick promptly said, "Yeah, he swung at the wild pitch. It was a strike."

"Then let's get it right," I said.

At this point, Mark Grace smiled and said, "Yeah, I swung."

Don Zimmer, the Cubs manager, watching intently, sensed we were now going to change the call.

Out he came, saying, "You can't change it now—they've got to protest before the next pitch."

It was true. The protest has to be made before the next pitch. Furthermore, even though my partners saw Grace swing, the rules state that someone—not necessarily the catcher—must ask for a second opinion. My partners could not, on their own, correct the call on the wild pitch.

Maybe it was a bad rule, and this was the kind of play to make the Rules Committee rethink it. But for now, the appeal was too late, and the count stood at two and one.

It really was no big deal, and it didn't affect the game. Afterward, no one even came by our locker room to ask about the play.

It wasn't until later that evening that I found out what a big deal NBC had made of it. They were assuming that I had screwed up, and their cameras were focusing on me and my ball-strike indicator for most of the rest of the game. They replayed the three pitches to prove it was one and two, not two and one. I was amazed to learn what a big deal they'd made of it. It was true; I had missed the swing. And it was true, the wrong count was allowed to stand. But the only people who really screwed up were the Pirates for not asking for assistance from the base umpires after I notified them all, quite clearly, that it was a two-and-oh count.

I think if Tim McCarver, a former catcher, had been announcing, he would have grasped what happened much sooner and explained it to the viewers. But it was just one of the crazy things that seem to happen in Wrigley Field and nowhere else.

CHAPTER ELEVEN

The Managers

NO QUESTION ABOUT it, umpires go head to head with managers more than with players, and a good reason for that is that managers consider it part of their job to get it on with the umps. They think that their players, their fans, and especially their owners expect it.

Even mild-mannered people, like Bill Virdon, know that it's expected that they get out there and argue like hell on behalf of their players, both to show support and to prove to the owner that they are "leaders." The smart ones can handle this job with dignity and not get all the umpires in the league mad at them. We understand their need to put on a show now and then.

I've certainly had my ups and down with Tommy Lasorda over the years. One night I ran him from a game for arguing too long, and the next day he walks out toward home plate to exchange lineups with his back to me. I'm looking at him and wondering, "What's going on here?"

Suddenly he turns around and he's got tape all over his mouth. And I knew he was laughing behind that tape.

I once told Roger Craig of the Giants to stop wav-

ing his arms at me so much from the dugout. I suppose
it was no big thing, but it was getting to be an annoy-
ance. So the rest of the game, he kept his hands in his
pockets; never removed them even once, making sure
I'd notice. The funny thing about Craig was that he was
always fair with the umpires when he managed in San
Diego, but he changed a lot when he got the Giants job.
I suppose when you get into the hunt you get a little
tougher, but it surprised me. Roger talks very slowly.
Argues the same way. He came out once and told me
I'd called a play too quickly. So I said, "No I didn't,
Roger, I took my time." So he answered, "Well, maybe
you did, but you still blew the play," You would call
that being prepared to win an argument no matter how
his first approach was received.

Dick Williams, when he was managing in Montreal, got thrown out one night, and was still boiling the
next day. Now you have to understand that even with
all of his success—he won pennants in three different
cities—he was not what you'd call a beloved figure
among his players. He was never accused of being "Mr.
Warmth."

He was so mad on this occasion that he wouldn't
even bring the lineups out himself. I think he knew that
he'd take one look at us and start arguing last night's
plays all over again. So he sent his pitcher Bryn Smith
out, and the first thing Smith says to us is, "Any chance
of throwing him out again?"

Sparky Anderson, when he was at Cincinnati, was
the best. You might throw him out one night but he'd
come back the next day all smiles and friendly and "how
are you gentlemen all doing today?" He might even say,
"You got me last night," just to break the tension.

Sometimes managers might have things on their
minds other than baseball. Certainly if their own con-

tracts haven't been renewed and it's late in the season, or if the newspapers are filled with rumors about them getting fired, you know their heads aren't always on every pitch. Who could blame them?

Chuck Tanner, who usually had pretty good job security, considering his profession, walked out with the lineups on the last day of the season one year. It was a nothing game for both teams. All I said was, "Hi, Chuck, what's goin' on?" And he looked at me in front of my three partners and cursed me in two words. I don't know what that was all about, but I had to run him, and he wound up getting fined $250. He got notified the day before Christmas. He never let me forget that Christmas present that he blamed me for.

I consider Whitey Herzog to be the best manager in the National League—I think most people do—and I go back with him to the days he was the Mets' farm director and a frequent visitor to the Instructional League when I was umpiring there. Whitey really knows each man's talent, and he can combine motivation with that knowledge to bring out the maximum in every one of his players. It's really an education to watch him work. And with his added abilities at making good personnel moves—like the year he came up with Pedro Guerrero and Tom Brunansky—he's really something extraordinary.

Years ago, back in the Instructional League, I was umpiring a game and he was observing the Mets' rookies. There was a soft foul tip and before I had a chance to say anything, the Tigers' catcher called it foul.

One thing you learn in umpire school—and you teach the players—is that the umpire makes the call, not the catcher. Herzog, just sitting in the Mets' dugout on a hot day in the Instructional League, heard the catcher say foul, and then heard me repeat it. He was

up in a second, getting on me for letting the catcher call
the play. I saw even then that nothing got by this man.

Years later, working a Cardinal game, with Whitey
managing, we're in the top of the ninth with the tying
run on third, and Todd Worrell is on the mound for St.
Louis. There are two outs.

Worrell came set, didn't pause, and delivered.
"Balk!" I yelled, and in came the tying run.

My partner John Kibler looked at me as if to say,
"What the hell are you doing?" but he knew that you
call those things from the heart, and you can't pause to
think about the score or the inning. A balk is a balk
whether it's the first inning or the ninth. Oh, man, was
Kibler pissed though. Not to mention Worrell, not to
mention Herzog. And do I have to tell you that we went
fourteen innings before it ended? And the Cardinals lost
it to boot.

Well, this would have been a fine opportunity for
Herzog to rip me apart in the newspapers, which I kind
of expected. After all, when he came out to argue over
the balk call, he said, "What the hell are you doing?
You're a better umpire than that! I know it was a balk,
but jeeez. . . ."

But all he said in the papers the next day was "That
Eric Gregg's a pretty good umpire . . . a little heavy,
but good."

When Joe Torre of the Mets called me a meatball
sandwich, I ran him out of there, but I went down the
line to tell my partner Frank Pulli what it was all about.
We were laughing about it, and Torre complained to
the league office about us laughing. The next time we
were in New York, Fred Fleig called me in and asked
if I was really laughing.

"Oh no, Mr. Fleig," I said. "I have white teeth and
a black face." He said, "Good answer. See ya."

One time I got permission from the league to wear a microphone during a game for a television special. Herman Franks was managing the Cubs. He'd been mad over a check swing by Mike Schmidt the night before. You can't argue that call when it happens or it's an automatic ejection, so Herman had been up all night seething about it and waiting to get on me the next day.

He started arguing about the play, but I interrupted him to tell him that I was wearing a mike for a TV special. I thought it was only fair.

He looked at me, smiled, and said, "Everything I just said I'm taking back." And he walked away.

Right after I'd lost over a hundred pounds and started a new season with a sleek new look, Jim Frey of the Cubs resumed picking on me. He used to pick on me about my weight, but now he was confronted by a new lean and mean Eric Gregg. All he could think of to say during out first argument was "Even though you lost all that weight, it turns out you still can't call them right."

Jerry Coleman was a broadcaster who managed San Diego one year. A lot of people thought that was a joke, letting a broadcaster manage, but many people forgot that Jerry was a star infielder with the Yankees for many years, and a very clever baseball man, the kind of guy who usually does wind up managing. The year he managed he got Lanny Harris to change a call during a game in New York—a balk call I believe, which is almost impossible to protest. But Coleman knew of some rule interpretation and he won his argument, which is certainly an unusual thing.

Bill Virdon, as I said, was the classic example of a mild-mannered guy who seemed out of character when he came out arguing. He managed Pittsburgh, Houston, and Montreal in our league. Sometimes, as a matter of pride, all he really wanted out of an argument was for you to admit you made a mistake. Never mind changing the call, just admit that you blew it and that would be enough for him. Of course, you'd never do that, so he'd go back to the dugout in a pout. He really did have a way of trying to embarrass you, but that was just his style. He'd come out and say, "Eric, I know my man was out because you called him out, but fifty thousand people here know he was safe. What are you going to do about this?" And in the end, he'd just want you to apologize.

Of all the managers I've worked with over the years, I guess Pete Rose is a very special case. As a baseball fan, I always had a fondness for him, as did all fans. He was a guy of limited abilities who wound up with more hits than Ty Cobb. Think about 4,256 hits for a minute—it means you get two hundred hits for twenty years and still come up short. What dedication!

I was at third base the day that Pete's forty-four-game hitting streak came to an end. He struck out his last time at bat. The next day I went to him and said, "Pete, if that was me umpiring back there, I'd have called that a ball."

"Really?" he said.

"Yeah, but you swung anyway." I laughed and walked away. He was a little mad about that.

I felt for Pete in 1989. He did his best to keep his focus on his managing job, but the gambling stories were all over the place by opening day, and he was determined to do his job and ride them out. I worked the Reds' opener, and when Pete came out to a big ovation with the lineups, he said to me, "How ya' doin', Eric, you look great!" I looked at him and said, "Me? How *you* doin'?" He was doing his best to keep his spirits up.

A few days later I called Chris Sabo out at third base. Pete yelled at me, "You're oh-for-one, Eric." The whole game, he kept getting on me. Another close play, and he yelled "oh-for-two," then came an "oh-for-three," and "oh-for-four." Why I'm buying all of this I don't know, except that there's a touch of humor to it somehow.

Then I had to call a half swing from third base and it went against the Reds too. Pete comes out of the dugout and says, "Eric, that's oh-for-five." Now I'd had it. I said, "Pete, are you done?" He said, "Yeah." I think we both knew what was next. I said, "Fine, you're gone."

Of all things, he comes after me now and says, "I'll bet you were wrong all five times." I looked at him and said, "Pete, you can't bet."

Through all he went through with his legal battles and the commissioner's investigation, he was still an easy-to-like kind of guy, and you had to feel sorry for him, even if most people believed and expected the worst. And then, to no one's surprise I guess, he was banished from the only thing he'd ever known in his life, baseball. The game lost Rose and, nine days later, Commissioner Giamatti. There were no winners here except the overall game of baseball, which survived a year-long pile of bad publicity over the Rose affair, and came out proving that no player was so big he could bend the rules to suit himself. I'll miss Pete, but Giamatti did the right thing, and I doubt that the new commissioner, Fay Vincent, will ever overturn Giamatti's legacy.

CHAPTER TWELVE

The Commercial

THE MOST FAMOUS commercial I ever did was one I wasn't in and had nothing to do with.

Huh?

Let me explain.

In 1987, I was watching a winter sports event with my oldest son and all of a sudden, here comes a Budweiser commercial about a black umpire, toiling in the minors, a dog running on the field, an ol' clubhouse attendant giving him a telegram, a call to the Mrs. from a pay phone, and then a game in Busch Stadium, an argument where a grizzled manager tests the rookie ump, and winds up buying him and his wife a Bud at a restaurant.

It was a terrific commercial; probably sold a few cases of Bud too. And it was very well done, all except for the dog running onto the field, because that never really happens. That, plus you get a phone call, not a telegram. But it was otherwise very accurate, and one thing was certain—this was my commercial. That was me in there, the black umpire. It was my story. Of course, we're not permitted to do beer commercials while we're still employed by baseball, but everyone knew it was me.

And everywhere I went, fans talked to me about the "Eric Gregg Commercial." Some people actually thought it was me, although the actor was just a bit more trim than I am. How funny it was that the commercial helped make me famous, and I didn't know anything about it until I caught it on TV.

I do enjoy television work when it does come to me. I like being interviewed, and I like doing the interviewing, and I had a terrific experience doing Phillies Franks commercials a few years ago; we must have done eight or nine of them. People still talk to me about them. That's the power of television. People still call Joe DiMaggio "Mr. Coffee," but I think he stopped doing those commercials ten years ago. In Philadelphia, so many people still know me for the Phillies Franks commercials, and of course, when the players would see them, they'd say it only proved what a hot dog I always was.

The way they came about was that John Kibler had done a commercial for Phillies Franks on the recommendation of Bill Giles, the Phillies' owner. The second year, Giles recommended Doug Harvey. In the third year, Frank Pulli took the phone call on the subject and just said, "Let's let Eric do it; he's from Philadelphia." And so that started a six-year association with Phillies Franks, which included not only the commercials, but also banquets and needless to say, all the franks we could fit into the freezer.

In the winter of 1983 I broke my ankle outside my home when I slipped on the ice, and it caused me to miss the first few weeks of the season. No sooner was that in the newspapers than the Phillies Franks people rushed a new commercial on with me recovering from the fall. Thanks to that commercial, I had one of the best-known injuries in Philadelphia sports that year, and got cards from hundreds of fans.

I once had an offer to appear in a music video with Terry Forster, the overweight pitcher whom David Letterman called a "Big Tub of Goo." It would have been a fun experience, I'm sure, but I quickly got word from Chub Feeney that I wouldn't get permission to do it. He'd been on me to lose weight, and this would have been like a slap in the face to those efforts. So, out went the $2,500 I was going to get paid, and my chance to make music video history with Forster.

After the 1989 World Series, I was invited to appear on a week of *Family Feud* programs, teamed with four other umpires against Joe Carter, Ozzie Smith, Wally Joyner, Rick Sutcliffe, and Ellis Burks. That was great fun and a nice taste of Hollywood.

CHAPTER THIRTEEN

The Players

MAKE NO MISTAKE about it—I'm a fan. Being right there on the field with all the greats of the game who have passed right before my eyes over the past dozen years has been a treat, and I've never lost sight of what a grand opportunity it's been for me. I wish I could have been one of them. I'm glad that I have done what I've done so that I can at least be a part of the national pastime.

I've got my favorites. I'm totally impartial when it comes to making a call, but that doesn't mean I can't admire an all-time great like Rose or Schmidt, and it also means I can have my favorites who are just good guys. And my dislikes for guys who are not my favorites.

Take Dave Kingman for instance. Bad guy. I was never alone in thinking this; most players agreed too. Kingman could have this holier-than-thou attitude problem. If home plate was a little dusty when he'd come up, he'd say, "Hey, take care of the housekeeping down here." He'd say that and I'd be dying for a nice mean slider over the outside corner so I could ring him up. I'd never intentionally call one against him, but I'd love it when I could call him out on strikes, especially if he'd look bad taking it. I'm human.

One year I vacationed after the season with my wife in Hawaii. I was lying out on the beach, when Kingman walks by, also on vacation. You'd think there'd be some friendly greeting, given the coincidence of bumping into me so many miles from home, but all he said was "What's a whale doing on the beach?" and he kept walking. I mean, it was in front of my wife. Anyone else with even an ounce of class would stop and say hello and let me introduce my wife. What a jerk.

When I go to the Dominican Republic to visit my wife's family, I always run into players. Some are retired, some are playing winter ball, some are vacationing. But it's always a nice warm greeting that we exchange when we see each other. We're all part of the same industry and away from the heat of the diamond, we're all brothers.

During the season you occasionally run into players, coaches, and managers in restaurants. Walt's Hitching Post in Cincinnati is a place like that, although usually you try and avoid places where the players like to hang out. But usually it's all good fellowship. Tommy Helms, the former Reds coach, might walk into the Hitching Post, see me at a table and say, "How many racks tonight, Eric?" That scene in the Bud commercial with the manager sending over drinks—that stuff happens a lot, especially in the smaller cities like Cincinnati where there aren't that many restaurants to choose from.

I guess umpires get closer to catchers than other position players for obvious reasons. You get to know those guys real well over the years: their habits, their likes and dislikes, even a lot of personal stuff.

When Steve Carlton was in his prime with the Phillies, he'd always like to have Tim McCarver catch for him instead of Bob Boone. While Carlton may have liked that, it bothered the umpires a lot, because Boone was a delight to work with, and McCarver, late in his career, was getting old and couldn't really crouch down well over a full game. That happens to older catchers and it's a burden to home plate umpires. I suspect Boone himself is now a victim of that in the American League. And Fisk and Sundberg and Dempsey. Catchers seem to be lasting longer these days with the shortage of good ones coming along.

The "high crouch" makes it hard to see the pitches properly. I finally had to tell McCarver to stay down or I'd bite his head off. He told me, "You do that and you'll have more brains in your belly than you do in your head." Boom, out he went and we got Boone in there. But it was a funny line. I'm not surprised he turned into a successful broadcaster.

Bo Diaz, there was a strange catcher. We didn't speak for two years. Imagine that. He got mad over some call and a two-year relationship, which had been very pleasant up to that point, ended just like that. When he needed a new ball he'd just hold his hand behind him without a word. And for my part, I refused to give him the count. He'd have to look at the scoreboard. It was a bad situation.

When Manny Sanguillen would have a dispute over a call, all he'd say was "Me no say nuthin'." He was an amazing hitter too. He'd swing at all the balls and take all the strikes. I never saw anything quite like it.

Tony Peña, who catches on one knee all the time, has a style all his own, but that's not what makes him famous among National League umpires. It seems he has this problem with, uh, passing wind. I mean, he could just destroy you if you unfortunately were calling pitches behind him. Watch umpires behind Tony Peña sometimes—you'll see time-out called a lot, and the umps walking away just to clear the air. You'd walk away, shake your head, and the fans would never know what was happening.

One day I'm working behind Tony. Since I'm bilingual, I sometimes take it upon myself to help out the Latin players with their English. No charge, just a friendly service.

On this particular day, Tony questions one of my calls. In English, he says, "Where the hell was that pitch at?"

Not being one to let bad grammar go uncorrected, I called time-out and said, "Tony, Tony, you can't end a sentence with a preposition. You can't end a sentence with 'at.'"

Cool as anything, Tony turned around and said, "Okay, where the hell was that pitch at, asshole?"

You can't throw a player out for looking at you funny, but if you could, Joe Morgan would have been thrown out of more games than he played. He'd just work you over with the meanest looks if he didn't like a call. Steve Garvey would give you a sarcastic grin, but Morgan had just the meanest look. And he'd get on me about "taking care of the brothers," like I was supposed to give black players better calls than white players. Crazy to expect that, just crazy. He told me once that "Garry Maddox thinks you're trying too hard against us so people wouldn't think you were one-sided." I have to admit that Morgan made me think about that for a long time before I realized he was nuts.

One of my toughest moments on a field came when I had to be a peacemaker during a serious fight in Cincinnati in 1986. Eric Davis of the Reds stole third. Ray Knight, the Mets' third baseman, must have thought there was something evil in the slide or something, and he wanted to start a fight. So he started shoving Davis.

I stepped between them—I was the third base umpire—and suddenly I grabbed Davis and put him in a full nelson so he was helpless, unable to fight. And now Knight starts pounding Davis, I mean, pow, pow, pow, he's hitting him. And I'm holding Davis! Something's wrong here. Finally I let go and the fight is under way.

Before you know it I'm getting letters from all over the place. The fight was on every newscast in the U.S. that night, and there I am holding Davis. Most of the letters said, "Next time, hold the white guy."

The next day when I saw Davis, he said, "How could you do that to me?" But the answer of course was that I never expected Knight to be hitting him once I was holding him. And then Knight saw me and said, "Thanks, Eric." Oh, that made me feel terrible.

The only thing that saved the situation for me were letters from Chub Feeney and Peter Ueberroth complimenting me for the way I stepped in.

Dave Concepcion was another guy who was always looking for a call to go his way, like we were soul brothers. And I'd have to remind him, "Dave, you're not even black, you're Latin!" I think he got even with me one year when he recommended a nightclub to me called "Limelight," or something, and I went there only to discover that it was a gay bar.

You had to like a guy like Jay Johnstone, who just brought a terrific attitude with him every day at the park. Anybody who can get released in 1973 and still be playing twelve years later is a survivor and the kind of guy you've got to admire.

My best encounter with Jay took place in Dodger Stadium. I was umpiring at second. Jay was with the Cubs. He hit one off the centerfield fence, Rick Monday fielded it and threw to second. It was like an automatic tag play, and I called him out. The problem was, Jay was safe. I saw it with my eyes, but my arm reacted to the automatic call. So my arm was in the out position, but I yelled "Safe!"

"Well, " Jay said, "what is it, safe or out?"

"Jay," I answered, "you and I know that you were safe. But there's fifty thousand people here who saw me call you out, so out it is."

You know what he did? He laughed and ran off the field.

One day, Greg "The Bull" Luzinski was up for the Phillies. Greg was the strong, silent type; never argued much, never said anything much at all.

I'm working the plate and the one-oh pitch comes over the outside corner and I yell, "Strike one!"

The Bull looks at me like I'm crazy, but he doesn't say anything. Now comes the next pitch, right around the same spot, and I yell, "That's two!"

He raised the bat over his head with those huge tree-trunk arms of his and says, "Two? Two what?"

I took one look at him and said, "Too high," and Gary Carter, who was catching, laughed like hell.

I had J. R. Richard in his last game, which means I was the home plate umpire in the final game of this great pitcher's career. Of course, no one knew at that time it would be his last. He was at the top of his game, perhaps the best pitcher in the league. It was July of 1980, J. R. was 10–4 and had been the starting pitcher in the All-Star Game. But he worked only a few innings in that final game, and then he called me out to the mound. He said he was feeling a little lightheaded and asked if his catcher could wear gloves. He said he was having trouble picking up the signs. I said no, but that the catcher could wear white tape on his fingers, which we allow. But he couldn't continue beyond that inning. Little did any of us know of the time bomb inside his body. A couple of days later he had a stroke, and he never pitched again. What a tragedy. He was a great one. I read recently that he might try to come back and pitch in this new Seniors League for players over thirty-five. I hope he makes it there; I know the desire to prove he can still pitch must still be there, even after all of these years.

His teammate Nolan Ryan could put fear in a batter's heart, partly because he threw about a hundred miles an hour, and partly because he made a very loud grunting sound when he released the ball. It was hard enough to hit a hundred-mile-an-hour fastball, but who needed to hear the grunt that went with it? For the batter, it was matter of a few pitches once every forty-five minutes or so. For the umpire, it was 135 pitches a game, the same grunt, over and over. It could make you crazy. On top of this, not every catcher could handle Ryan. He was not easy to catch. Sometimes a fastball pitcher throws what they call a "soft" pitch, easy on the receiver. Not Ryan. Combine the speed with the touch of wildness, with the grunt and the heavy pitch he threw, and it was trouble. Poor Luis Pujols, he just couldn't catch him at all, which was murder on the umpires, who got whacked constantly back there.

Phil Niekro, even with that crazy knuckleball, was very easy to work with. The ball danced around so much that he wouldn't even argue if he thought you'd missed one, because it was very hard to tell even from his end. Just because it was a strike here, it might be a ball an inch later and then a strike an inch after that. I'd tell Niekro, "Hey, if Bruce Benedict can't catch it, how can you expect me to call it?"

A funny thing about Niekro was that he wasn't too

good on names. He knew I was Gregg but he didn't
know my first name, and once he had to use it on a
postgame interview that we were listening to on the radio. He called me Baron Gregg.

I don't know, maybe some players really believe
you call plays for them or against them. If they think
you're going to put your career on the line for any of
them, no matter who, they're insane. Still . . .

Keith Hernandez did an advertisement for sun-
glasses, so naturally, on the field one day that year, I
asked him if he could get me a a pair. In that game, he
hit a liner down the line, which I called fair. It was fair,
of course, but maybe Keith thought I'd given him one
because the next day there were three pairs of glasses
in my locker.

If umpires made short lists of special players, Rusty
Staub would probably have made most lists. Just a really
good guy.

I became famous among umpires for giving Rusty
the only heave-ho of his entire career.

On top of it all, it was his last season. Twenty-two
seasons, no ejections, and I got him in number twenty-
three. It was over a balk he wanted me to call on Don
Sutton in Houston. He wouldn't yell at the crew chief
for some reason, so he directed it all to me, and he
wouldn't quit. So I tossed him. George Bamberger, the
Mets' manager, came out and told me that it was Rusty's
first ejection in twenty-three years.

Word travels fast. I heard all the other umpires in
the majors couldn't believe the news. I didn't feel too
good about it either. I assumed everyone thought I'd
screwed up.

* * *

When Fernando Valenzuela came up in 1980, he was awesome. I don't think he had had any idea just how good he was, but the players and umpires knew. He had a brief shot in 1980 before his big Fernando-mania year in 1981, but even off that 1980 touch, word was spreading.

I spoke to Fernando in Spanish when he came up, as I often do with Latin players. Some Americans tell you to speak English to Latins or they'll never learn, and it's probably true, but I like to dust off my Spanish and make them feel comfortable. The Latin players always want to know if my kids speak Spanish. It's important to them. (They do.)

Fernando just isn't Fernando anymore, and that's sad. He still has his stuff, but he doesn't hit his spots anymore. He's not the same pitcher. He used to be able to hit the corner when he wanted to, but now the same pitch goes right over the middle of the plate.

I got into an embarrassing situation with Vince Coleman once. I asked him for a glove for my son Jose. He gave it to me, but the next time he saw Jose at Veterans Stadium, he remembered and asked Jose if he liked the glove. Jose said, "What glove?" Oh, did Coleman get on me for that one.

My kids loved Jose Cruz, a very underrated outfielder with Houston for many years. The kids love the way the P.A. announcer in the Astrodome pronounced his name. My kids have met a lot of players over the years, and by and large the players have always been great to them. It costs me a lot of money, but I send the kids to Episcopal Academy in Philadelphia, where Mike Schmidt's and Bill Giles's kids go. It's my wife's idea. She thinks we should spend our money on education, and when I see the results, I've got to say I agree with her. Plus, all I have to do is think of my brother and sisters and know how they fared without good educations.

I once had an argument with Reggie Smith of the Dodgers in which he brought up the name of Art Williams, the league's first black umpire.

"You know the difference between you and Art Williams?" he asked me in the middle of the dispute.

That got my attention, so I asked, "What?"

"Art Williams was a good guy."

"Hey, Reggie," I answered, "you know the difference between Reggie Smith and Eric Gregg?"

That got his interest. "What?" he said.

"Eric Gregg is still in this game," I told him. The rest of the sentence was delivered with my thumb.

Being such a close observer of the National League for more than a decade and a half, I can feel qualified to draw up some All-Star teams. I definitely can give you an All-Star team of general good guys, and, while I may not be the best judge of talent in the game, I work close enough to the action to have some pretty good opinions on All-Star performers. And spending idle hours compiling such lists is one of those beautiful things that baseball is all about.

My all-star team begins with Keith Hernandez at first base. Willie Montanez was a fancy fielder, but I go all the way back to the Florida State League with Keith, and he's just such a reliable gloveman who makes even the toughest plays seem routine. And even though they kept the game-winning RBI statistic for only a few years, Keith was the all-time leader, which proves what a clutch hitter he has been.

At second base, it would be Joe Morgan, despite all of those looks he gave me. Few second basemen had his power, plus he was fast and a great fielder, and to me, a certain Hall of Famer.

At shortstop, it's the Wizard of Oz, Ozzie Smith. He's done things no one ever thought could be done at that position, and I suspect that when he retires, the game will miss those skills more than it now knows. I'll always remember a play he made when he was with the Padres—long before the whole country knew about his abilities. He went out into the hole behind third base, barehanded a hard grounder, and got his man at first. What a play!

My third baseman is Michael Jack Schmidt, maybe the best ever at that position. I go way back with Schmidt, back to the days we lived next to each other in a little Travelodge motel in Clearwater during spring training before he even made the majors. He may be the last one we ever see reach five hundred home runs, and he could pick it at third and run the bases well. He became a complete player, something no one anticipated when he first arrived on the scene.

In left field, I've got Tim "Rock" Raines. He too has that great power and speed combination, but his comeback from drugs is very inspirational, and I'm influenced a little bit by my admiration for that. No one would doubt that he's been an outstanding player.

My center fielder is Tony Gwynn. Awesome is the word. He just hits pitches that other players don't even make contact with. And he can put them in holes you didn't even know were there. He's almost impossible to defend against. As he gets on with his career, people are starting to appreciate his defense too. Just a great player.

In right field, it's Andre Dawson. He finally got the

respect he deserved when he went to the Cubs. A lot of people appreciated him in Montreal, but somehow players up there just don't get the notice that they get in New York, Chicago, or Los Angeles. The Hawk has got a great arm and the ability to swing the bat, and he's my right fielder.

My catcher is not Johnny Bench, but Gary Carter. He's the best I've ever seen, and believe me, we get to work very close to all the catchers. I've been with Carter since I had him in the Eastern League in '73, and he's always been a great all-around player.

My starting pitcher is J. R. Richard. I put him ahead of Seaver, Carlton, Gooden, Ryan, Valenzuela, all of them. He had something none of them had—that little wildness that just made hitters plain afraid to step in against him. He might walk two or three guys and then he'd strike out the side. He threw the hardest slider I ever saw. What a shame it was that it ended so suddenly for him.

My relief pitcher is Bruce Sutter, the master of the split-fingered fastball. He was always all business on the mound, as though to say, "Here's my best pitch, go ahead and hit it." And no one could. He was always ahead of the hitters, the key to being a successful relief pitcher.

My manager is Whitey Herzog, who has the respect of just about everyone in the game now as the best active manager. I don't believe that there's anyone who handles situations better than he does, not only for a knowledge of the game, but for an instinct to know when to make a move, even one as small as arguing a call.

As for my good-guy team, I start with Willie Stargell at first base. Pops is probably the captain of the team. He would never lose his composure, and always enjoyed his time on the field. Once I called a strike on him that was so high it could have brought rain. He looked at me for a second, but never said a word. He had so much style.

At second base, it's Manny Trillo. He loved it that I had a Latin wife, and as much as he got on me, it was always good-natured and pleasant. Poor Manny had only one ejection in his entire career, and that was me. I called him out on strikes, he threw his bat and cursed me, and I had to run him. But the next day he just laughed about it and things were back to normal.

At shortstop, it's Garry Templeton, the guy the Cardinals traded to San Diego for Ozzie. I've never seen him show up an umpire; he was a class act all the way. I know he had his problems in St. Louis, but never with me.

My third baseman is again Mike Schmidt. I had only one argument with Mike in all the years we were together, in 1989, in his final weeks as an active player. He was arguing a call and I told him to knock it off, because he was showing me up.

"You're showing yourself up," he said. But I knew it was frustration on his part. I knew he was coming to the end of the line, and he knew it too.

Mike was always one to ask me about new umpires. What were their names, where did they come from, who did they replace. And he'd talk about umpires with me, like "Doug Harvey's been calling the inside pitch on me this year—he never did before," and things like that.

In left field I've got Greg "The Bull" Luzinski. He just beats out Greg Gross. What a nice man. All the umpires like Luzinski, and he always made sure he'd say hello to you every day.

My center fielder is Dale Murphy. I remember when he came up as a catcher, I worked behind him and he said to me, "I love being in the big leagues, but I sure don't like catching." Eventually, he became valuable enough to the Braves for them to accommodate him and move him out of there and into the outfield. Dale's always been a great guy, even when he's started to struggle in the last couple of years.

In right field, I've got Rusty Staub, another guy like Trillo who only had one ejection in his career, and it was from me. I like Rusty's restaurants in New York too.

My good-guy catcher is Bob Boone, even though he's been in the American League for a long time now. He'd always let a young umpire umpire. He'd tell you next week if he though you missed one. And he'd give you a real good look at the pitch. Some people say he'd "frame" a pitch by moving his glove ever so slightly, but Boone was a class act who worked with the umpires. He'd catch with his palm down, and give you a really good reading of the pitches. And he'd let the game unfold without breaking your concentration in the first few innings, when it's important to get your timing and your concentration down.

My starting pitcher is Steve Carlton, whom most writers found uncooperative. But he was so easy for umpires. He threw strikes all the time. Once I called two balks on him in a game and he never said a word, although he looked at me like I was a little crazy. Basically, he was a quiet warrior. He'd never say "great game" or anything, because, like an umpire, he just went out and did his job.

My relief pitcher is Kent Tekulve, whom I had in the minors as well. I'm a good low-ball ump, just right for his delivery, and he was overpowering with that sidearm stuff. Another class act.

Finally, for all of our ups and downs, my good-guy

manager is Tommy Lasorda. When all is said and done, he's just been a great ambassador for baseball, as I hope someone might say of me someday. You have your days with Tommy, but he still has so much fun in him that you can't exclude him from the good-guy team. And no one is better at getting his players psyched up for the game.

CHAPTER FOURTEEN

My Colleagues

THE ONLY PEOPLE who know what's it all about are my colleagues. And the amazing thing about our little profession is that we get assigned to four-man crews at the start of the season and stay pretty much intact all year, never seeing each other unless we happen to pass in an airport. But somehow, we maintain a bond. We know what's happening with each other, and when you include our days of learning in winter ball, instructional school, the minors, spring training, and Umpire Development School, we've all worked with each other at one time or another and all share the common brotherhood.

I think someone typical of the umpiring professional was Dick Stello, who died in 1987. He was a class act. He taught me a lot, including off-the-field behavior. He even gave me one of his best suitcases, just handed it over and said, "Here, use this," because he said I wasn't packing correctly.

Dick was married to a stripper named Chesty Morgan. She didn't get her nickname for those big brown eyes. One evening he took us to one of his wife's shows.

I guess you have to understand that Dick was raised

174

in show business, was a great singer himself, and to him, this was show biz. Of course to us, his three partners, this was very different. The opening number was a riot: Chesty comes out on stage led by two midgets, each holding aloft one of her finest assets. It was a riot, but here we were sitting with her husband. What were you supposed to say under the circumstances? Hey, nice boobs? The most amazing thing was going backstage with Dick after the show to meet his wife, and all of the other strippers strolling around, naked and almost unaware of the visitors. It's still one of the strangest nights of my life.

Dick died at age fifty-three when he and a friend stopped along Route 33 in Florida to put a tag on a car they'd just purchased. Another car, swerving to avoid a crash, plowed into him. What a waste.

The Dave Pallone story was like a soap opra. I always thought he was a gutsy umpire. We went to umpire school together and had been partners on and off over the years. We were together in 1988 when he had this big argument with Pete Rose that led to the beginning of the end for him.

The Mets were in Cincinnati on April 30. I had called a balk on Tom Browning that sort of got things rolling. This was the so-called "year of the balk," and managers were starting to tire of it. Rose, though, good guy that he was, had invited me to be his guest at his restaurant after the game. But even with the balk call, he told me, "That's okay, you're still taken care of at the restaurant." A few more balks, all called by Pallone against the Reds, followed. Things were getting tense.

In the ninth inning with the score tied 5–5 and a Met runner on second, Mookie Wilson grounded to short. Barry Larkin's throw to first pulled Nick Esasky off the base and Pallone called Wilson safe. Howard Johnson raced home with the go-ahead run when the arguing began.

Rose ran onto the field after Pallone. Dave was a scab umpire, but we have never let these guys hang themselves. We've always protected them. But Rose got there fast, and before you knew what was happening, he pushed Pallone twice.

When Pete's gambling problems came out the next year, people said, "How could he not have known the rules?" But it was the same thing with Pallone—he certainly knew the rule about shoving an ump.

Anyway, Pallone ran Rose, as he should have. As Pete was leaving the field, he yelled to me, "Forget it, Eric." I knew there went the restaurant. But he was also yelling, "He hit me, he hit me," because Pete knew he was in big trouble.

The fans started throwing things onto the field—dangerous things, like cigarette lighters, transistor radios, and batteries. Pete is beloved in Cincinnati. You run Rose in Cincy and look out. It's like throwing the pope out of St. Peter's Basilica.

With all the debris coming flying down, the four umpires left the field and went to our locker room. We sat there mostly talking about the play, which Pallone got right, and how crazy Rose had acted. We stayed in our locker room for fifteen minutes, which represented fifteen of the longest minutes I've ever spent in baseball.

When we went back on the field, it appeared that Pallone was now being singled out for a further showering of junk from the stands. Somebody threw a hot dog out that landed at my shoes. I thought for a moment about eating it, but the timing just wasn't right.

Pallone left the field. The newspapers reported that

John Kibler, our crew chief, instructed him to leave. That wasn't the case. Pallone left on his own without consulting us, which was an unthinkable situation. If he'd said to Kibler, "John, I can't work under these circumstances," Kibler would have forfeited the game against the Reds and that would have been the way to handle it. But he didn't consult anyone. He took it upon himself to leave. From that moment on, he was held in very low regard by his fellow umpires, even lower than his entrance as a scab in 1979.

As for Rose, he was suspended for a month by Bart Giamatti, the National League president, and fined ten thousand dollars. That served as a warmup for their bigger problems over gambling a year later when Giamatti was commissioner.

As for Pallone, he was back with us the next day, but things were tense between us. He received death threats, he had a conference with the commissioner, and my other two partners were concerned about the threats. They could easily have been mistaken for Pallone by some crazy Reds fan. They decided my problem wasn't as serious as theirs, since I was less likely to be mistaken for Pallone. The FBI got involved and once again said, "Don't worry, people who are out to get you don't send death threats." But it was serious stuff. Pallone resigned before the end of the season, and then during the winter there came stories linking him to sex crimes (they were dismissed), and the report that he was off to write his own book in which he would describe his homosexuality. This was news and it wasn't. It was one of those stories you hear where you'd never thought about it, but hey, now that you mention it. . . .

Anticipating your next crew is one of the things that make the winters drag. It's a critical assignment be-

cause you're practically married to your three partners
for the next six months. The American League always
seems to make its assignments earlier than the National.

I've worked with just about everyone by now. Some
you get along with better than others. When you're a
crew chief, you can pick one partner. I'm close with
Frank Pulli, and when he becomes a chief, I think he'll
choose me, which I'm very much looking forward to.

Frank is one of those umpires who will call a play
with his heart, not just his head. Anybody can call a
balk with the score 10–2 in the sixth inning. The mark
of an umpire is one who can make that call with the
score tied in the ninth. Frank can pull the switch in that
situation. He's got the guts. Not everyone does.

When I first came up to the majors, I thought you
had to be loud to make your presence felt. Now, with
more seasoning, I've come to realize that respect doesn't
come with the loud call. Besides, you run out of gas.

Sometimes, you anticipate a call, like that Jay Johnstone play in Dodger Stadium I mentioned earlier. Joe
Garagiola calls them "neighborhood calls," as in, if the
ball's in the neighborhood, the guy's out. The kind of
thing Al Barlick would never subscribe to. Players understand this aspect of the game. One day Tim Raines
slid into second and I called him out. He said, "Eric,
he never tagged me," but I said, "Timmy, I know that,
but the ball was there."

I remember one day in Philadelphia making a call,
and I'll be damned if I knew whether it was right or
not. So I turned my back and waited to hear footsteps
coming up fast on me to argue. But, no footsteps. So I
said to myself, "Eric, I guess you got that one right."
Later my wife asked if I was sure if I had that play right
and I said, "Of course," but I had no idea.

When I watch a game on television, I'm not watching it like a fan, I'm watching it like an umpire. I'm calling the pitches to myself, checking out the umpires I haven't seen in a while. It's one way we "keep in touch." Do I ever second-guess an umpire after a replay? Sure, just like everyone. But I love replays. They make the umpires look great.

People sometimes say they should have television replays in baseball to judge close calls. Well, not only will that waste a lot of time in proving that the umpire is right 99 percent of the time, but it will also be far more inaccurate than a live umpire right on top of the play. Camera angles distort things a lot. Take the center-field camera shot. Does the pitcher look anywhere near sixty feet from home plate? It's very distorted.

Besides, baseball isn't like football where the play stops after the official blows the whistle. In baseball, a lot still happens after the call. Say it's a play at first. Action isn't automatically halted. Runners can keep moving. What happens if an instant reply reverses a call? What do you do with the runner who kept going based on the umpire's call? It's far more complex than any football situation in which the whistle halts all action.

Doug Harvey, the senior umpire in the National League, adds a great deal of distinction to our profession by his manner and his abilities. He knows that some people call him "God" behind his back, but hey, if you can't handle a little name-calling, you're in the wrong business.

I was on a flight with Doug once and it may have been the only time he came close to losing that great dignity. We were in a terrible lightning storm and the plane was being rocked around like none of us had ever experienced. It was about three o'clock in the after-

noon, but it looked like the the middle of the night outside. A woman sitting in front of us tried to make humor
out of it, but Doug yelled at her to shut up, which was
really out of character for him.

Then at one point Doug put his hand on mine and
said, "Kid, I think I may have called my last strike."
That was a fairly frightening thing to hear from a guy
they call God.

We made an emergency landing in Cleveland. We
somehow found our way to this redneck bar across the
street from the airport. In the bar is this one big guy,
about six-seven, and what do you know, it's Tim
McClelland, an American League umpire. I said, "Tim!"
and he looked up and said, "Eric Gregg? What the hell
are you doing here?" I told him we'd just had the worst
flight of our lives, and Harvey was across the street in
a hotel, calling his wife and settling his nerves.

John Kibler, my sometime crew chief, is a very
punctual guy, very well organized, and not a guy you
want to antagonize. He had a heart attack in 1983, his
son was in a serious auto accident three years later, and
you don't like to upset John. So one day in Chicago,
when we made up to go to Wrigley Field together, well,
maybe he should have selected someone else. You see,
I'm not the most organized guy in the world. And at the
appointed time to meet in the hotel lobby, I hadn't even
begun to pack my bags yet.

John called my room and I said, "Sure I'm packed—
be right down," but I was not even close to ready, and
John was getting annoyed. He knew I was lying, I'm
sure, and by the time I got downstairs, he was in our
rental car, and I had to start running after it to explain
myself and catch up. I guess we were like Felix and
Oscar, the Odd Couple, but if you picture me throwing

everything into my suitcase, shirttails hanging out the sides, you can picture what a scene we played out together.

Punctuality isn't Nick Colosi's big thing, but "The Snake" is one of the cleanest guys you'll ever meet. He was a head waiter at the Copa in New York. His son worked for an airline. Believe me, they knew how to use the old knife and fork. He's a sight to see on a flight. If we're getting bad service, he'll just ask the stewardess to come over, and calm as anything say, "Pardon me, may I have your name?" She'll catch on quickly and soon it's, "Oh, Mr. Colosi, is there anything we can do for you?" At a party one day, I saw him carry four plates and four drinks in one hand. Like Lasorda, Nick knows Frank Sinatra and drops his name when the occasion calls for it.

The late Lee Weyer was six-six and about 250 pounds, but he had a squeaky high voice that he could throw like a ventriloquist, and he could drive a stewardess crazy calling her name. She'd look all over the place for a little boy who needed her.

On July 4, 1988, Lee died of a heart attack at Ed Montague's home in San Francisco after working a game at Candlestick Park earlier in the day. He was only fifty-one. Lee had been in the league since 1963, and he even came back from a nervous system disorder in 1980, Guillain-Barre syndrome, that affected his coordination and eyesight. He also suffered from diabetes. A good man. A tough loss.

On September 22, 1988, Barney Deary died of a heart attack in Tampa after attending a meeting of baseball farm directors. He was in his car when he apparently felt chest pains. He got out and attempted to get help, but he never made it. He was sixty-two.

Barney was a tough old marine, a World War II veteran, and very much a father figure to all the rookie umpires who went through Umpire Development School. He and his wife always made me feel so welcome in their home after I'd graduated and gone on into pro ball.

Barney had sort of been retired by baseball not long before his heart attack; at least he was being phased out. I don't know all the politics behind it, and maybe after nineteen years it was time for someone else to run the program, but I'm sure he wasn't happy about the reduced work load. He was a dedicated servant of the game.

I regret to this day the falling out we'd had in 1979 when he had to supply scab umpires during the strike. I understood, my partners understood, and I'm sure Barney hoped we understood. Had he taken a stance of refusing to help, he'd have been fired, and what does a broken-down umpire do at fifty-three? I guess any of us might have acted the same way. And I'm sure Barney understood our determination at that time and the need for unity and the feeling about the scabs. He did what he had to do, we did what we had to do, and it was a tragedy of the situation that it put a wedge between the old teacher and his graduates. One can blame the circumstances more than the people involved.

Still, I loved the man and I wept when I got the news. I was in San Diego and called the league office to see if they'd excuse me to go to the funeral, but Ed Vargo, our supervisor, said he couldn't do it because if he let me go, he'd have to let everyone go. The truth was, not that many really would have gone. The feelings over the strike were still there. Since I didn't get permission to miss work, I flew all night to visit Barney's widow in Florida, paid my respects to her, and flew out the next morning in time to work the game that night in San Diego.

Barney was a class act, an able administrator, a top-rate teacher, and a confidant to us all. I asked him if I should marry Conchita. He told me to do it. As usual, it was good advice from the old master.

Like many who make up baseball that the fans never hear about, Barney Deary was one of the behind-the-scenes people who made the game possible. His death barely made the newspapers, but the news came hard to those who loved him.

CHAPTER FIFTEEN

The Life

DON'T GET ME wrong—I was never lacking in self-confidence, and I have no doubt that I'm an outstanding umpire. If I had any doubts, I'd be in the wrong business, because there is no room for that once you're on the field.

But I'm also smart enough to know that not everyone agrees. Because I like to have a good time out there, because I can be a little more colorful than baseball has been used to, some people think the flashiness gets in the way of my work. It doesn't, but I know it's been said, and I suppose it's worthwhile to be aware of it.

They've always said that umpiring can be a lonely life. It's just four guys, traveling together all year, staying in different hotels from the players, not fraternizing with the other members of the "industry," away from home and family for extended periods. And hey, it is all of that. But for me, it's always been a little lonelier, and a little more removed. Being black is one reason of course. Not only am I in such a minority, but my colleagues are not generally thought of as the last of the liberal Democrats. By and large, the umpires are conservative, salt-of-the-earth guys, traditional in American

184

values, flag-waving patriots—the sort of people you'd want on your side if the going got tough. None of that is intended as criticism. I'm a live-and-let-live guy, and there's plenty of room for all kinds in the country as long as we tolerate each other. I'm just making the point that I wasn't exactly umpiring the annual softball game at the NAACP picnic.

Also, I'm younger than most of my brethren, and always have been. I got to the majors at twenty-six, and even after all of these years, I'm still among the younger umps. And I know that there are always, and will always be, people who think I made is so young because there was pressure on the league to promote a black umpire. I'm not naive about the whispers, but I can sleep very well at night knowing I'm good at what I do, no excuses necessary.

My outgoing nature also produced a lot of friends and a lot of perks on the road. I might get a car or a suite when others don't, and I'm not ashamed of it, but I know not everyone thinks it's right, something about not knowing "my place."

I also get more banquet and commercial opportunities, and that's probably resented a little, but hey, there's nothing wrong with that. This is America, after all.

I remember being in Baltimore one winter for a banquet, and they sent a beautiful white limo to the hotel to pick us up. I was there with Johnny Mize, Brooks Robinson, and Frank Robinson. Being there with Frank was a little difficult, because he was always so tough on umpires. In 1989, he threatened to resign because of the way the umpires were treating him, but that's just Frank. He's always had his problems—at Cleveland, at San Francisco where I worked many of his games, and at Baltimore.

Anyway, Mize and the two Robinsons got in the back, and I had to sit in the front. This is a British limo, with the driver, who was white, on the right. I'm sitting where the driver ordinarily sits. And every time we stop at a traffic light, the car next to us does this triple take, first seeing the stretch limo, then seeing the black guy driving (me), but then realizing I'm not driving; the driver is white and he's over there. And in the back, Frank is laughing his head off. This may have been the only funny moment I ever had with Frank Robinson.

I've been to Ken Kaiser's big banquet in Rochester a few times. Ken is the Eric Gregg of the American League—their largest umpire. Funny guy, too. Only man I know whose car has a bumper sticker that says, "Honk if you're carrying groceries." I could have made a fortune that weekend at the hotel where we stayed. Everytime I stepped outside, someone would hand me their bags. They all thought I was the bellman. One girl said to me, "What do you do if you're not the bellman?"

I thought for a second and said, "I'm here for a banquet. I'm a jockey for Clydesdales."

I once went on a banquet tour with Doug Flutie, Phil Simms, and Mickey Mantle. We flew a small charter plane, and you had to get weighed before you got on. I asked why that was, and they explained that if you weigh 275 you have to sit here, if you weigh 300 you have to sit here, and if you weigh 325 you have to sit here.

As Simms, Flutie, and Mantle looked on, I had to say, "What if you weigh three seventy-five?"

They all started laughing like hell and one of them said, "You get the next flight!"

That little tour was an amazing experience, because I got to see firsthand what life was like for Mantle. Let me tell you, a great guy, and very accommodating with fans, despite the fact that his reputation wasn't always like that. He was terrific. But the poor guy never got a break. We'd get to a hotel, and the dash from the cab to the elevator was a nightmare for him. He's so easily recognized that someone always spots him, grabs anything handy, and bolts after him. Suddenly everyone in the room is on top of him, and he's praying for the elevator. It comes, they all get on with him and plead with him to sign, walking all the way to his room. Then of course, word gets out what room he's in, and the whole thing becomes impossible. He finally had to quit the tour just to get away from this.

Me, of course, I'd sign anything, and was always happy to be asked. But one day there was this one kid who got my autograph on a ball, and came back later to show me how he had to erase it, because Mantle had also signed and he didn't want to ruin the ball by having me on it too.

Going to these banquets is a lot of fun, because I enjoy meeting people, and that's what you do at these. They are usually arranged as fund-raisers, either for civic organizations or charities, and we get paid appearance fees. You go to cocktail parties with the other dais guests, which is where you really get to meet them, then the dinner itself includes some speeches, and usually some autographing afterward. To some people, especially the really big star athletes, it may get monotonous and repetitive, but for me, it's still just another part of being associated with Major League Baseball, and each one is a real kick.

My life at home in the winter is pretty normal, almost dull. I usually get up early and get the kids ready for school so Conchita can sleep in. I'll whip up some bacon and eggs, hot cereal, milk, whatever. I'll sit and watch *Sesame Street* with my little babies, then go off

about 8:30 to work out, always trying to keep the weight
down or lose some more. It's not always easy, especially on stormy wintry days in Philadelphia, but I've
got to keep at it or it'll get away from me. About 10:30
I go to the University of Pennsylvania where they let
me swim for about an hour. For sixty minutes, I'm an
Ivy Leaguer. I go home, watch *The Young and the Restless,* my favorite soap, pick up the kids at school, get
them off to choir practice, help out with dinner, play
soccer or basketball with the kids, get them bathed, ready
for bed, and I nod off myself about 11:30. I don't know
how Conchita does this by herself all during the baseball season, but she's great at it.

A few years ago I had the pleasure of visiting the
set of *The Young and the Restless* and meeting the cast.
I had been on a flight with a member of the CBS crew
who worked on the show, and he arranged it. What a
thrill that was for me. I visited again in 1989 and brought
Conchita with me. When you watch these soaps day after
day the characters are a part of your life; the actors are
more the characters than they are themselves. I know
it's a little silly maybe, but people who put this stuff
down tend to be the "highly educated," who graduated
with lofty degrees, and get just as much pleasure out of
classic novels, and hey, what's really the difference?
Fiction and fantasy, we can all use our escapes, and those
soaps have gotten me through many long afternoons,
waiting for night baseball games. Over the years, I've
also been a big fan of *Search for Tomorrow, Days of
Our Lives,* and *Another World.* It wasn't always easy to
remember which characters and which plots went to
which soap, but you work at it.

My musical tastes run to jazz, but I also enjoy Michael Jackson, Bruce Springsteen, and Stevie Wonder.
I'm not much of a country music fan, but Joe West, the

N.L. umpire, is just terrific at playing the guitar and singing songs like "Take This Job and Shove It," or "You Picked a Fine Time to Leave Me, Lucille." When you see something performed in person, it gives you a greater appreciation.

I've always been very proud to be a National League umpire. For many years, the National League was the superior league in terms of playing talent, although the American League has come back a long way toward reaching parity. It's been said that one of the reasons for the National League superiority in All-Star Games was their early entry into the signing of black players, beginning with the first, Jackie Robinson. I know that even as an umpire, I owe Jackie Robinson a debt; without Jackie's breakthrough, and the way in which he handled it, there would be no black umpires today either.

I recently came upon an amazing bit of information which really puts in perspective that theory about the National League getting the jump on signing great black players.

Of the sixteen black major leaguers in the Hall of Fame, only one—Satchel Paige—was signed by an American League club. The others all began in the National League—Jackie Robinson, Roy Campanella, Roberto Clemente, Monte Irvin, Ernie Banks, Willie Mays, Bob Gibson, Hank Aaron, Frank Robinson, Juan Marichal, Lou Brock, Willie McCovey, Willie Stargell, Joe Morgan, and Billy Williams. Not until Rod Carew and Reggie Jackson get to Cooperstown will the American League finally have their first long-term players inducted. And Carew wasn't signed until 1964, eighteen years after Jackie Robinson. Jackson was drafted in 1966.

* * *

As much as I love umpiring, I've never denied for a moment that I would have rather been a player. If I hadn't been a third-string catcher in high school, well maybe. But it just wasn't in the cards.

One year though, 1985, with the development of the so-called "Fantasy Camps," I decided to try life on the other side. I went to Clearwater, Florida, the home of the Phillies' spring training camp, and put on a uniform to be a player for a week. It was a tremendous experience.

The first day out there, I was fined four dollars for skipping the intrasquad game because I was doing interviews with the press. Not a great start.

Then, in my very first game, I hit into a double play, mostly because it took me the better part of a day to get to first base.

I was up the next time with a man on first, and I thought the pitcher balked. So I politely questioned the balk call by the Fantasy Camp umpire, and while we didn't have an argument, and I never stopped smiling, the irony of the situation was obvious. I was getting my shot at arguing with the umpire after all those years.

One day I left camp to become an umpire again— for a sequence being filmed at the Mets' Fantasy Camp for *Saturday Night Live*.

But I had the time of my life that week, and although it was all in fun and filled with laughs and good times, it was interesting to cross the line and see how the other half lives. When you're bearing down, trying your best, and you *think* the umpire has blown a call, it's pretty easy to see how your frustration can come out. I always knew it, but it made me understand it just a little better. It was a very valuable experience.

One problem with life on the road is the occasional medical needs you develop, and the necessity of finding a strange doctor or dentist to help you. In such cases, you usually turn first to the home team's trainer, who has a good listing of where to go. I had a crazy thing happen in spring training 1989 in St. Petersburg. A foul ball jammed into my mask and knocked out my front tooth, the one that had been a cap since I was eight. Now I was in a mess. You can't get along without a front tooth. You look ridiculous, and you can't speak properly.

I spent most of that spring trying to get it repaired. The temporary cap they put there required a special glue, and of course, one day I forgot the glue. I was umpiring a Kansas City game when I called a balk on Charlie Leibrandt, and my cap popped out. George Brett caught it in his glove, turned around and said "What's this, your tooth? You lost a tooth calling a balk? Take it easy, Eric!"

We had that big "Year of the Balk" in 1988. The balk rule is difficult for fans to deal with because balks are so hard to see. Half the time a fan is not even concentrating on the pitcher at the moment the balk is committed. It is something that again highlights the umpires' need for total concentration. We can never take our eyes off the pitcher once he's preparing to deliver the ball. As for all of the 1988 balks, nobody was particularly happy about calling them, but we had our marching orders. I'm pretty sure it all began with the World Series of 1987. The broadcasters were all talking about Bert Blyleven not coming to a full stop, and I think my boss, Bart Giamatti, was influenced by this. He wanted the game to be played by the rules (naturally), and the more he heard the broadcasters getting on Blyleven's delivery, the more he became determined to enforce this in '88.

I'm not a guy who calls a lot of balks, and I didn't really change much in '88. If there's such a thing as a "good balk umpire," it would be the guy we call "Bee

Oh Bee," Bob Davidson. I say this because although he calls a lot of balks, he's very consistent, and can never be questioned for calling it one way one time and another way another time. As for me, I didn't call them unless it was a clear violation of that full-stop rule, unless the pitcher was cheating to prevent a stolen base. But I backed Mr. Giamatti, because he was the boss, and a good one at that. He really made an effort to get around and get to know us all, and we respected that. He was the only one to tell me that I had to trim down or it might cost me my job, but he backed it up by making sure exercise equipment and access to workouts were available all season long. Of course, I'd be on the exercise bicycle and then I'd have a few burgers, so I didn't always get the full benefit out of the workouts. But I tried.

I had Bill White's "debut" as league president, when he threw out the first ball in Cincinnati. It was amazing to see that this former Gold Glove first baseman threw like a girl! John Kibler had told us about it before the game; he had umpired when Bill was still playing. Sure enough, Bill threw funny, and talked about it to the writers. He said he'd always thrown like that, but it was a funny sight to see.

Before I got the 1989 World Series assignment, the most historically important games I'd umpired were the Pallone/Rose game, the 1986 All-Star Game, the League Championship Series in 1981 and 1987, the first night game in Wrigley Field, and my only nine-inning no-hitter, Tom Browning's perfect game of 1988. I was at third base that day, but it was a thrill to be on the field to see that happen. The amazing thing was that when history was almost made in 1989—when Browning came within three outs of becoming the first pitcher in the history of baseball to throw two perfect games, I was once again at third base. Had he done it—and I sure thought he was going to—I would have been a great baseball trivia answer for years and years to come.

I almost had my first no-hitter as a plate umpire in 1988. David Cone of the Mets went seven and two-thirds innings at Shea Stadium and up came Steve Jeltz of the Phillies. He turned to me and said, "I'm gonna break it up," and sure enough, he got a ground ball through the infield and did. It wound up being a two-hitter for Cone. How about a hitter like Jeltz being so bold and coming through? What a game.

Technically speaking, I do have another no-hitter in the history books, and in fact, another perfect game. The date was April 21, 1984. We were in St. Louis for a doubleheader with the Montreal Expos on an overcast day. David Palmer was the Expos' pitcher in the second game, with Eric Gregg behind the plate. Palmer had missed the entire '83 season with an elbow operation, and this was his second start since returning to the big leagues.

Amazing as it seems, Palmer set down the Cardinals for five perfect innings. Fifteen men up, fifteen men down. And then the rains came heavily in the top of the sixth. We'd already sat through an hour-and-a-half rain delay in game one, and the field was pretty sploshy, even for artificial turf. I don't know how Palmer felt about the prospects for continuing—whether he wanted to go for the full nine, or settle for a perfecto in a shortened game. My guess is that after a long delay, a pitcher's rhythm usually changes, and the odds were against his getting the next twelve in a row. This was a good-hitting Cardinal team too, with Andy Van Slyke, Lonnie Smith, George Hendrick, and Willie McGee. As the rains came down, it was apparent that we couldn't resume play, and that was it—a perfect game in the history books.

There are probably not many people around who can tell you that David Palmer once pitched a perfect game, but he did. I was there. But the circumstances just weren't right. There was no drama, no final out to celebrate, no heartbeat racing as all eyes focused on Palmer. All we had was a long rain delay.

I worked in left field in the 1986 All-Star Game at the Astrodome, a game won by the American League 3–2, which was the one Dick Howser managed just before he had to leave baseball, ill with cancer. It was also the game in which Fernando Valenzuela struck out five straight. Frank White's homer to left center (my call) was the winning run. It was certainly strange to be a left field umpire, and I couldn't help but think backward in my career to the minors and even to Little League, when it was all done by one umpire.

The 1981 National League Championship Series was my first taste of six-man umpiring, and my first taste of postseason play and postseason money. It was the Dodgers against the Expos, won in the final game on Rick Monday's ninth-inning homer off Steve Rogers. I worked the plate in Game Two at Los Angeles when Ray Burris shut out the Dodgers on just five singles, beating Fernando in his sensational rookie season.

The '87 League Championship Series was the seven-game classic between the Giants and the Cardinals. It was the Giants' first LCS in sixteen years, and they hadn't won a pennant in twenty-five years. But they lost the last game 6–0 to end their hopes. I was the home plate umpire in the fourth game at San Francisco, a double complete game by Danny Cox and Mike Krukow, and when do you ever see that anymore? In fact, it's the only double complete game in National League Championship Series history, hard as that is to believe. The

Giants won 4–2 on homers by Robby Thompson, Jeffrey Leonard, and Bob Brenly.

For special memories, though, the first night game at Wrigley was really something. First of all, I had never been able to see *The Young and the Restless* in Chicago before, all the games having been day games.

August 8, 1988 was the date, and they even took a group shot of the umpiring team amidst all of the festivities. The park looked like the World Series with all the flags and bunting, all the politicians and media on hand. I read that there were 556 members of the press there. As it happened, the Cubs got off to a 3–1 lead when heavy rains forced us to stop play. We waited two hours and ten minutes and finally called the game, which meant that the next first night game ever in Wrigley Field was the following day, a 6–4 Cub win over the Mets without all the fanfare. But for a regular season game, I never saw such excitement. It was an honor to be a part of it.

I had two other special days in recent years: one, my 20th high school reunion, and the other, a day the public school system of Philadelphia honored me in 1989.

The high school reunion was just tremendous. Since I still lived in Philadelphia, I knew a lot of people, but some I hadn't seen in years. Baseball fans knew about me and about my weight, but to some, seeing ol' "Hub" in a size 50 jacket was a little on the surprising side. They asked me to be a speaker, and I did my regular routine of umpire stories. I introduced my old girlfriend Marcelle and said, "Marcelle, if you knew back then that I'd be making a hundred thousand dollars a year now, I think you would have tried a little harder to marry me."

I was very moved by the honor the school system

gave me. It happened early in the '89 season, and I got a day off from the league office in order to go home for it. I was named the Outstanding Graduate of the Year in Music and Dance from the Philadelphia school system. Those old days of harmonizing on street corners and being in school plays all came back to me. A lot of my old teachers, including Joe Goldenberg, my coach, showed up at the downtown Dance Theatre, along with about five hundred other people, to see me get the honor. It was a very, very proud day for me, and if I have to say so, a very proud day for the Philly school system too.

The awards program read:

HONOR GRADUATE AWARD

Many graduates of the Philadelphia Public School System go on to successful post high school and post college careers, often with significant impact on the lives of young people through their support or activities in education. Many such individuals have demonstrated time and again those qualities of personality and character which have inspired young people and the community as a whole.

This year the award is given to:
ERIC GREGG
National League Umpire (since 1978)
Graduate of West Philadelphia High School

Professional and/or Community Accomplishments
Wall of Fame—West Philadelphia High School
National Baseball League
Officiated 1986 All-Star Game
Officiated 1981 & 1987 Championship Series
Member of Boys Club of America & numerous
community organizations

Every day is not spent just rubbing up baseballs with Lena Blackburne Baseball Rubbing Mud out of a coffee can in the umpires' clubhouse. You really never know what's waiting on the field, what piece of baseball history you might witness, or what you might yourself be walking into. Most umpires may be invisible to the fans, and they say they're the best kind, but the game is a long way off from being officiated by robots, and the four humans surrounding the diamond in dark uniforms can put a lot of the human touch into any game.

CHAPTER SIXTEEN

Quaked Out

THERE WAS NO truth to the rumor that the San Francisco earthquake of 1989 began when I slipped in the shower. But that's what Giants' manager Roger Craig jokingly accused me of only minutes after the quake hit Candlestick Park. And it turned out to be not a very funny thing.

I knew exactly the week in which World Series assignments would be coming out for 1989, and it was no secret among those who knew me that I was going to be very let down if I didn't make it. I felt my turn had more than come around, that I should have been selected by then.

The phone rang in my hotel room in Houston on September 15 at 2:30 in the afternoon. I was watching my soaps.

I recognized Bill White's voice. I'd spoken to him a few times since he became league president, but I really knew his voice from the days he broadcast Yankee games. Sometimes I'd watch them in New York if I was working a Mets series and the Yankees were playing later in the day.

"Eric, I know this is something you've always wanted," he said, "so I'm happy to tell you you've been picked to work in the World Series this year."

"All right, that's great," I said.

He couldn't tell me who my partners would be yet, because he hadn't notified them, but we have a good grapevine among ourselves and within a few hours I learned that Paul Runge and Dutch Rennert from my league and Rich Garcia, Al Clark, and Vic Voltaggio (in his first Series) from the American League had been selected. It would mean I would clear about an extra $4,700 in pay, along with a cherished World Series ring.

The Series would honor the memory of Bart Giamatti, and our uniforms would have a special designation to commemorate his brief term as commissioner. Little did any of us know that we were walking into a chapter not so much of baseball history but of American history.

So for the first time in my career, when the regular season ended I went home, not to be an observer of the World Series, but to watch the playoffs with the knowledge that my work was not yet over.

I did not have a real rooting interest in the League Championship Series, other than thinking that it would be nice to have Oakland and San Francisco win so that I could settle down in one hotel for the whole week. But that really wasn't that big a deal. I thought it would be special for the Cubs to make it after so many years, and the city of Chicago was really lit up in excitement and anticipation. But it was not to be. Oakland defeated Toronto for its second straight American League pennant and San Francisco beat the Cubs for their first National League pennant in twenty-seven years. The Cubs would have to wait.

I wanted my two oldest boys, Jose and Kevin, to go

with Conchita and me to the Series, and that turned out to be more of a task than I expected. The Episcopal Academy does not have its great reputation for education by accident. And they were not at all impressed by the idea of having the boys miss school for the games. Negotiating this one took a great deal of the week, but in the end, after I promised to make sure that the boys got their assignments in advance and returned with all of their homework done, the headmaster gave his okay.

Conchita was going to bring her sister along, and I had one other thing I wanted to attend to. I wanted both my mother and my father to come with me.

My dad had not seen a baseball game in over ten years, not since that day at the Vet when I looked up and saw him in the stands, and they put it in the Phillies' highlight film. And, since he didn't drive and didn't get out of the house much, he seldom spent much time with his grandchildren. This would be a special occasion for the Gregg family and I wanted him there. I also wanted my kids to spend time with their grandparents—both of them. Although Mom and Dad had not traveled together in thirty years, they were not hostile toward each other. They had shared in the tragedy of Cheryl's death. My dad had shown concern over Mom's illnesses. They were not getting any younger and it would mean a lot to me to have them together one more time, as my career reached its zenith. I used all of my powers of persuasion and made it happen. Mom and Dad were going with us. It was my dad's first flight.

The World Series was to begin in Oakland on Saturday, October 14. I flew out myself on the 12th and checked into the Westin Hotel near the San Francisco Airport to get everything arranged. I had the Presidential Suite on the seventh floor where we'd all stay. Mom and Dad, Conchita and my sister-in-law, and the boys came out on Friday. I rented a van for the week, and was now delighted that we could really unpack and avoid any travel during the series.

San Francisco and Oakland. A classic matchup. Two cities that during the decade of the eighties thought they could no longer support major league baseball were now hosting the World Series. The excitement was everywhere, especially around the hotel where all the hotel workers were talking about it throughout the day.

I crossed the Bay Bridge to Oakland on Saturday and headed for the Coliseum. There was a feeling in the air unlike any I'd ever felt before. I never saw such activity in the umpires' locker room. Not even the All-Star Game, when Vice-President Bush visited, really approached this. The FBI was there, the two league presidents, Richie Phillips, representatives of the commissioner's staff, umpiring supervisors Ed Vargo, Dick Butler, and Marty Springstead, photographers, Oakland Coliseum officials—and this was only the umpires' room! I couldn't find a place to sit.

I was glad that in my first game I would be working the right field foul line. I looked forward to the quiet that I'd find there in the vast grassy area, away from all the chaos of the locker room.

Prior to game time, the two managers, Tony LaRussa and Roger Craig, visited with us. I was amazed to see the conversation turn to Dennis Eckersley's pitching style and whether he "cheated."

LaRussa looked at Craig and said, "Roger, you know me, you've known me a long time, and I tell you, he doesn't cheat." And Craig said, "Okay, Tony, I believe you."

I couldn't believe it. It was so gentlemanly. All the brutal arguments I'd had with people over the years over whether a pitcher was cheating or not, and here were these two men, on the verge of the games of their lives, simply reaching a calm, gentlemanly understanding before they were even confronted by Eckersley coming into a game.

One other subject came up—the ground rules for the Coliseum. These had to be reviewed not only because the Giants had never played there, but because extra seats and other alterations had been made to accommodate additional fans.

We got to the ground rule about balls going into the bullpens. It read, "Ball going into bullpen bench, and rebounding onto playing field: In Play. Ball remaining on or under bench: 2 Bases."

Someone in the room groaned as it was being read. "Hey, this is the World Series," said Craig. "Let's try not to have a ground rule stop the action and maybe decide a game. The fans want action, not play halted."

Additional discussion went on. It was finally agreed that unless the ball rolled into a ball bag or was totally unplayable, it would remain in play. Everyone in the room—the six umpires, the two league presidents, and the two managers—was in agreement. A ground rule should be the last resort with a championship on the line.

There wasn't much further discussion on that, as we moved on to other things, such as jewelry. More and more players had taken to wearing gold chains around their necks. We told the managers to have the players tuck them it; otherwise, they'd be a distraction, and we'd ask them to be removed.

Commissioner Fay Vincent came in and congratulated each of us for being selected for the World Series. He was very professional and very much on top of his job. There was no way of knowing that this was his first World Series as commissioner, and in fact, his first World

Series as a baseball official. I wanted to ask if he'd ever been to a World Series as a fan, but I thought it might sound disrespectful. But this was my first, and I wondered if it might be his as well.

We talked about the number of warmup pitches a pitcher would take between innings. The American League usually allowed five, the National League eight. I said to Bobby Brown, "Hey, if TV wants two-fifteen for commercials, why should we make the guy stop warming up?" So we all agreed that eight pitches would be allowed.

The subject moved to disabled players on the bench. The Giants wanted Dave Dravecky there for inspiration. He was the pitcher who came back from cancer to pitch again in 1989, only to break his arm in his second turn on the mound, and then again while celebrating the Giants' LCS victory. A decision was reached to permit an equal number of ineligible, disabled list players to sit on the bench for both teams.

Now it was time to head to the field. The ceremonies were lavish and I had a growing excitement as we lined up for the national anthem. It seemed for a moment that I was back fourteen years, standing there at my first major league game, telling Satch Davidson that I wanted to scream out loud. I thought of West Philadelphia High, the Little League games, umpire school, Barney Deary, the Dominican games, the New York–Penn League, the Instructional League, the Florida State League, the Eastern League, the Pacific Coast League, and everyone who'd been so helpful to me. I stole a look at my family, sitting over on the National League side of the field, and took it all in. I was about to umpire a World Series game.

I went out to right field and had a fairly quiet game. Candy Maldonado of the Giants said "congratulations" to me as he took his position, but Jose Canseco was quiet and all business.

Between innings, early in the game, Paul Runge wandered out to me and brought up a trapped ball situation. I don't know what made him do it, but he was probably thinking of things that could come up, and how having two extra umpires would help.

"I've been thinking, Eric," he said, "that on a trapped ball play, it would be a good idea for both of the outfield umpires to cover it, because you can never be sure in advance who the outfielder is going to be and which hand his glove is on and whether the glove would smother your vision. It might be that the ump on the other side could get a better view than the man nearest to the call."

No sooner did we have that conversation than bang, that very inning, a sinking liner fell in front of Canseco, and I had the call. It was exactly the way Runge described it: Jose's glove, on his left hand, made it impossible for me to know for sure whether it was a catch or a trap. For a split second I feared that I wouldn't be able to make a call; then it squirted out of his glove for all to see. I was lucky. But you can be sure that Runge and I exchanged a smile after that one.

Running off the field after the game, I said to Canseco, in Spanish, "So, you're the big guy." And he was big; awesome, in fact. He may be the dominant player for the next decade in baseball if he stays healthy. I guess there will be some question of that after an injury-ridden 1989 season. He smiled back at me and acknowledged that my Spanish was pretty good.

The second game, if you believe ABC and the press, featured the one umpire screwup of the Series, and they spelled it GREGG. I'm still burning over the treatment I got in that game.

It was the seventh inning, I was in left field, and Rickey Henderson hit a ball that rolled into the bullpen like it was part of a pinball machine. It kicked off the side of the wall, squirted under the Oakland bench, and landed on a towel. It was not wedged out of reach, and was playable. I was right on top of the play, remembered immediately the change we had made in the ground rules, and I gave it a clear palms down sign to indicate it was "in play."

It wasn't my fault that Giants' left fielder Kevin Mitchell decided to stop chasing it. Nor was it my fault that Rickey Henderson slowed down in confusion as he approached third. As umpire Al Clark told me, "Eric, you were right on that—your mechanics were flawless. Everyone in the world could see that the ball was in play."

To call it a ground rule double would have taken all the excitement out of the play. It should have been the most exciting play in the whole World Series—an inside-the-park home run for Rickey. But I knew we had changed the ground rule and I was right all the way.

As I later discovered, ABC really let me have it. Al Michaels, Tim McCarver, and Jim Palmer looked up the ground rules, shared them with the audience, and told everyone that Eric Gregg blew the call. With all of the money that ABC puts into broadcasting a World Series, even with two extra announcers, Joe Morgan and Gary Thorne, on field level during the action, they had neither the ability nor the motivation to check this out. And it was obvious that the press was not informed of the change by the Commissioner's Office.

How could they have hung me like they did when Roger Craig didn't even argue the call? That was the most telling thing of all! Did they think that Craig, in a World Series, would let Henderson have a triple instead of a double? Roger knew the rule. Yet they never bothered to find out what really happened.

They weren't alone either. *USA Today* and some local newspapers called it "an error by Eric Gregg" the next day. As far as I know, only Stan Hochman, writing for my hometown *Philadelphia Daily News*, came to my defense with a column.

This was no small matter to Richie Phillips. The ABC attack was a slander to the umpiring profession, and the fact that baseball did not have a mechanism to correct them was a serious flaw. Phillips took it to the top—to Commissioner Vincent.

We were told that Vincent had arranged for ABC to make an apology to me and our crew during the pre-game telecast of Game Three.

The only problem was, the pregame telecast got quaked out.

Candlestick Park. Game Three. October 17, 1989. I was at third base for this one, more likely to be part of the action. It was a National League ballpark, a familiar site, but they turned the umpires' locker room into the postgame interview room and assigned the six of us to two small locker rooms down the hall. I was with Rich Garcia and Paul Runge. Richie Phillips was looking for me before the game and wanted to know which one I was in.

"The one with the food," he was told.

It had worked out that way.

We had all gone onto the field around five P.M. to survey the changes in field level seating. I happened to look at a clock as I returned to my locker room. It was 5:02.

Two minutes later, the ground began to shake. I knew immediately what it was. You can't visit San Francisco without giving at least a little thought to the earthquake situation. When I learned later that the whole thing had lasted only fifteen to twenty seconds, it was hard to believe. I remembered so vividly my thoughts—knowing it was a quake—and my reactions—yelling, "Get on the floor or under the table!" And I remember Richie Phillips going crazy, and my yelling to him, "Get under the doorway." This was his first quake.

It was a frightening thing. I dove for the floor and tried to get under the table, but a lot of junk was crammed under it and I couldn't get all the way under. And Garcia had climbed on my back in panic.

When it was over, Phillips began yelling, "My wife, my wife," which got all of us into a panic and sent us outside in search of our own families.

I spotted my family right where they were supposed to be and motioned for them to come down to the field. Giants and Athletics players were also in search of their families, but there was no panic, no chaos. The fans and the police were absolutely terrific. It was amazing how orderly things were, and that kept anyone from getting overly emotional. I had two friends along with my family, seven people in all, and everyone was fine, except for my wife and little Kevin, who were the most scared.

In the ballpark, we had no idea of the destruction and loss of lives outside. We were shut out from communication due to the power going out. The fact that the Bay Bridge and the Nimitz Freeway had collapsed, and that nearly seventy lives were lost within that twenty seconds was unknown to any of us at Candlestick. All we knew was that we'd had a good-sized quake, but we'd all survived. The ballpark didn't collapse, the fans hadn't panicked, and all seemed well. For a while, we even thought the game might still be played, but then it was obvious that that was out of the question.

And so one by one, everyone assembled their families and left the ballpark, uncertain what the plans were for playing the third game. I was the last to shower and change, which was not a bad move, because I was able to leave with all of the beer and soda that had been left in the locker room, along with a tray of shrimp that had to be worth a hundred dollars. I piled my family into the rented van and headed back to the hotel.

It was at that point that we began to realize how severe the damage had been. Highways were closed, power was out, and the traffic didn't move. For two and a half hours we sat in the van, until, exhausted and frustrated, we pulled alongside the road and ate all the shrimp and drank all the soda and beer.

When we reached the hotel it was nearly midnight, some three and a half hours after we'd left Candlestick. I had two small children up well past their bedtime, and we arrived to find that the hotel had been closed until it could be checked for structural safety. Only the ballroom area was open, and some people were being housed there whose homes had collapsed. As for the Greggs, I got all of the blankets and pillows I could find and right there on the front lawn of the hotel, I made some kingsize beds for us to sleep in. I set up a bed for the kids in the van.

At three A.M., we were told that we were allowed to return to our rooms. It was a seven-story climb, particularly difficult for my mom, but we made it. Inside our room, we were shocked to find mirrors shattered, vases destroyed, and no television reception. The radio, however, was working, and for the first time we heard about the Bay Bridge collapse.

It would be in the coming days and weeks that I'd begin to realize how lucky I was, for my family and for myself. It could have struck Candlestick and collapsed the upper deck, and I think if that had happened, one

could easily imagine twenty-five thousand deaths. It
could have collapsed on my family. Thank God that luck
was with us. And how awful it was for those whose bodies would be uncovered in the days that followed;
crushed in their cars because they'd had one more, or
one fewer traffic light on the way to their destination.

I hung around for a couple of days and then went
back home. Only Dutch Rennert and Vic Voltaggio
wound up staying in San Francisco. I didn't know how
to feel. This was my first World Series, but now, the
hearts of everyone involved had gone out of it. I wanted
it to resume, but even then, it would not have the same
atmosphere. I know I didn't want it to resume while
bodies were still being uncovered and have to share
news bulletins with that awful situation.

Some people said the Series shouldn't resume at
all. But hey, they didn't close the movie theaters, and
the newspapers didn't stop carrying comics and recipes.
Life had to go on, including the entertainment and sports
industries, because at times of trouble, they are possi-
bly more important than ever. People needed to know
that there was a spirit to move forward, to show that we
can continue where we left off. They played the World
Series during World War II for the national morale.
Surely they could play this for the morale of the Bay
cities.

As though I didn't have enough on my mind as I
waited out the days before the Series resumed, another
story broke that made it impossible for me to experience the rest of the Series with a clear head.

On October 25, a prison riot erupted at Camp Hill,
Pennsylvania, where 2,600 state prisoners were housed.
One of them was my brother Ernie.

Ernie was not a model prisoner, and had even done

some time in "the hole"—solitary confinement. He still
had about ten years to go on his long sentence for drug
and weapons convictions. We had no idea whether he
was a leader of the riots, or if he was dead or alive. We
knew there had been a lot of people hurt, and could
only hope that somehow he wasn't one of them.

The prison was designed to hold about 1,800 in-
mates, so you can imagine what the living conditions
must have been like for the 2,600 there. I'm not an ex-
pert on the penal system, but that must have been a
place waiting to explode. When the riots ended, half of
the prison's thirty-one buildings had been destroyed by
fire and 118 people were injured. It was announced that
744 prisoners were going to be transferred to other state
penitentiaries. We had no idea what Ernie's fate was.

This was all on my mind as I returned west with
Conchita.

San Francisco was like a ghost town. Usually, it's
alive with tourists, but this was no place for that now.
For those of us involved with the World Series, we were
sort of unwelcome tourists—there to finish a job, but
please, no merriment.

The hotels were empty except for Series-related
people and some in need of temporary shelter. I drove
over to Fisherman's Wharf, which was usually bustling
with visitors. There's a parking lot there that's always
hard to get into. The attendant told me to "park it anywhere." It was true, the place was deserted. When they
count up the billions of dollars of damage that hit San
Francisco, they probably won't even begin to measure
the impact on tourist dollars.

The detours all over the city prevented me from
seeing the areas where most of the destruction had hit.
But back east we had followed the cleanup and the res-

cue efforts each day, feeling particularly close to the people involved because we'd been there.

People seemed to be divided about playing. Most of the hotel workers I spoke with wanted the games canceled, but the 49ers played football before we returned, and that helped to establish that the sports industry would go on.

It was quiet in the locker room; somber almost. We went about our business, aware that the excitement had passed. It was obvious that this was now our profession, and we had a job to get done. It wasn't all fun and games with us along for the ride.

Tim McCarver stopped by. He was apologetic about the poor reportage on the call in Game Two. But the apology that was supposed to be made on the air never came. There was a moment in the fourth game when they had a long closeup of me at second base, and an opportunity existed, but they never made the apology or the explanation.

Game Three, played at last, was very moving. I was touched when they had twelve rescue workers throw out the first balls. One of them was a fireman I'd seen on television and after the ceremony I walked over to him to shake his hand.

The fans were all handed the words to "San Francisco," the "open your golden gate" song that I'd heard all my life. It was one of those songs where you only know those two lines, and then you go da-da-da-da with the rest of the lyrics. This time, you listened. It turned out the song was about San Francisco coming back after the 1906 earthquake, which had pretty much leveled the city. And to hear those San Franciscans raise their voices in a spirited version for 1989 was a tremendously uplifting moment. I'll never hear the song again without thinking of that. Whoever planned those opening ceremonies did a wonderful job, and the spirit that filled Candlestick Park after them made you feel as though we were all doing the right thing in being there. It was a message to the "outside world" that not only was baseball back, but San Francisco was back. And it was a great way to share it.

I didn't have much action at third or second in the final two games of the Series which the A's won to complete the sweep. I had one play in the fourth game where Canseco stole second. It was close but I called him safe. The fans booed.

They never show replays of controversial or close plays on the big scoreboards, but we now live in a time where many people bring battery-powered television sets with them to ballparks. In addition, people in luxury suites have televisions too. So you get conditioned to hearing a boo, then you pause while you know the replay is being watched, and you either hear a second boo, or nothing at all.

The Canseco call drew nothing. So I knew I got it right.

I didn't get to work home plate when the Series ended in four games, but I'll be there some other year. For now, I was glad it was over. I'd get home in time to trick or treat with my kids. There would be no "Mr. November" in baseball. We get paid the same whether it's four games or seven, so I got my money for working the minimum. And we were all uncomfortable finishing up the Series within just a few miles of places where lives had been lost.

I got home and continued to try and learn about Ernie. Richie Phillips, who is well connected, learned that he was not among those transferred, and was in general lockup, not the hole. That was a relief to us all, but a few days later, my mom heard from someone that the prisoners were all shackled and confined until the situation normalized, and that we might not have gotten the whole story. It may or may not have been true, but it was difficult not to know his fate. As much trouble as he'd had, at least we always knew he was in some way safe. Now we couldn't be sure.

With the news of the prison riot, it had to make me thank God once again for leading me into baseball. Ernie and Eric, two brothers, same environment, same parents, same opporunities. Ernie's looking at ten more tough ones, his body burned, his life ruined. Eric's looking for many more great days on the ballfield. He heard a promo on *The Game of the Week* to go to umpire school, and he left The Bottom forever.

Some people wondered if the Series should have gone on. "What's baseball," they asked, "at a time like this?"

For this one guy, it was only the thing that saved his life.

Index

215